"We are very proud of our growth and national standing with the other 'hot growth companies.' However, we feel that a great deal of Serv-Tech's success has come from the careful selection of its people, i.e., the advice, education, and assistance of Birkman & Associates."

Richard W. Krajicek, President
Serv-Tech, Inc.
Houston, Texas

"The simplicity and elegance of the Birkman® Questionnaire was a surprise to most of the people, especially when they read their feedback reports. Many people stated that they could not believe that such in-depth feedback could be derived from such a simple questionnaire. Even more impressive is that not a single person rejected the accuracy of his or her Birkman Report."

John Whitesell, Ph.D.
Kaizen Consulting
Canada

"The Birkman Method® is an excellent tool to provide unthreatening feedback to team members on personal styles and needs. Other methods provide surface information on style without giving you the tools to use the information to form more effective teams. . . . Several members of my team had individual personal insights which have changed their lives."

Marie L. Kotter, Vice President
for Student Services
Weber State University
Ogden, Utah

"I am still captivated by the incredible genius behind The Birkman Method® of measuring the soul. What a gift you are giving to all people."

Dr. Bruce Larson, Co-Pastor
The Crystal Cathedral
Garden Grove, California

". . . our group was in trouble. Interpersonal problems abounded; there was no respect for one another. I was driving people to conform to job descriptions, and some people didn't have the skill or desire to perform the job. The Birkman® process helped me to understand the people I work with; they are just people with needs."

Pam Urie, Human Resource Manager
Coulter Electronics of Canada, Ltd.

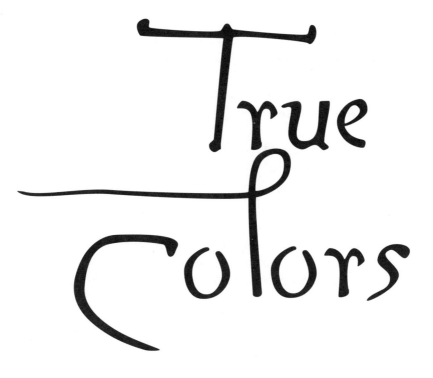

True Colors

ROGER BIRKMAN, PH.D.

Thomas Nelson Publishers

Nashville • Atlanta • London • Vancouver

Published in Nashville, Tennessee, by Thomas Nelson, Inc., and distributed in Canada by Lawson Falle, Ltd., Cambridge, Ontario.

Third printing 1997 by Signature Press, Inc., Houston, Texas.

Library of Congress Cataloging-in-Publication Data

Birkman, Roger W.

    True colors / by Roger W. Birkman.

    p. cm.

    ISBN 0-7852-7856-7 (pbk.)

    1. Birkman Method of Personality Testing. 2. Perception

  3. Psychology, Industrial. I. Title

  BF698.8.B47B57   1995

155.2'8–dc20

                                   94-36196

                                     CIP

1 2 3 4 5 6 7 — 01 00 99 98 97 96 95

This book is dedicated to the glory of God
who has taught me about the
uniqueness and complexities of relationships
and to all the people from whom
I have learned so much.

CONTENTS

1. IF AT FIRST YOU DON'T PERCEIVE 1

Even when your perceptions are accurate, are you making accurate assumptions as well? And what problems arise if you *don't?*

2. WATCH HOW YOU ACT! 13

How much of your behavior is primarily "for show"—to impress other people? Is there anything wrong with such behavior?

3. YOU AREN'T NORMAL 21

What's your definition of *normal?* Is your behavior based on what you know to be true, or on one of the many myths espoused by society?

4. WHAT'S YOUR COLOR? 37

Based on your knowledge of your own personality, can you predict where you would fit on our Life Style Grid? Will the results of our mini-questionnaire bear out your prediction?

ACKNOWLEDGMENTS

Years ago while employed by the U.S. Air Force as a research psychologist, I presented a philosophical view of the way behavior and motivational needs could be more easily understood, measured, and managed. At the time, I was unaware that these insights could also help reshape thinking about organizational change. This presentation was the beginning of a journey which has been both intriguing and challenging. Exploring the mysteries of personality diversities has been a joy and a privilege.

My acknowledgments must begin with the assertion that this is not "my book" even though my name is listed as author. More accurately, this is "our book," and I am deeply indebted:

To Stan Campbell for his writing and editing. His superb talent has made it possible for the accumulated experiences, concepts, and discoveries to be logically presented and summarized in readable form.

To Dr. Roy Mefferd, Jr., whose professionalism, scientific achievements, probing intellect, deep insights, and innovative thinking have made invaluable contributions.

To all employees of Birkman & Associates, Inc., past and present, who on a daily and yearly basis translate our mission and objectives into positive action.

To every business, personal, educational, and government client our company has had the privilege of serving. I regret that it is impossible to list each one by name.

To the managers, the organizational and human resource consultants, and the men and women of the private sector who shared personal experiences, insights, disappointments, and successes, I express my gratitude. Each has contributed immeasurably to this book.

My deepest thanks go to Sue, my wife. Her sustaining influence is present throughout the developments presented here. She was always standing by with her own considerable talent, sharing the mission and the dreams with never-failing support. Year after year she helped in the probing and the interpretation of the concepts. Her commitment and unselfish concern for the development of the methodology made the difference in its early survival. When the going was rough, she suffered through the defeats, the real-life struggles and pressures that are part and parcel of pioneering new views and theoretical assumptions.

ABOUT ROGER BIRKMAN

AND THE
BIRKMAN METHOD OF
PERSONALITY TESTING

If asked to list the modern psychologists who have become well-known by delving into the human psyche and sharing what they've learned with the general public, several names are likely to come to mind: Minirth and Meier, Buscaglia, Peck, Myers-Briggs, Trent, Smalley, and others. One that *isn't* likely to pop up in most circles is Birkman—at least, not yet.

However, Roger Birkman has been devoted to understanding personality and learning to evaluate it since most of his above-named peers were still in diapers. He is truly a pioneer in the exploration of human behavior. His fascination with the subject began during his college days prior to World War II, and his service as a fighter pilot during the war only piqued his interest. After the war, he returned to college to pursue a major in Psychology—a relatively new field at that time—and graduated with a Ph.D. from the University of Texas.

By 1950, he had developed a unique method of assessment designed to recognize and optimize human potential while teaching a healthy appreciation of one's self and an understanding acceptance of those who differ. In 1951, he founded Birkman & Associates in Houston, Texas. At that time the company consisted of himself and his wife. Today, consultants both within and outside the company are using "The Birkman Method" internationally in a wide range of personal and organizational applications.

In the more than forty years since the company was started, the primary concern has been both scientific and professional excellence. Literally millions of dollars have been spent in research to ensure that Dr. Birkman's system of assessment is simple to adminster, accurate in its results, widespread in its application, and scientifically valid. The database of people who have used and benefited from his work is quickly approaching one million. Yet much of this success has been due to word of mouth. This book is the first published product to take his finely-honed method of assessment beyond the corporate culture.

This book represents more than forty years' worth of thought, research, intense study, and firsthand application. It took a long time to create something so complex and complete, and then to simplify the process for ease in understanding.

So Roger Birkman doesn't mind that he may not yet be one of the most recognized names in the area of personality assessment. He lets his work speak for itself. And the word is spreading. For example:

• Several divisions of AT&T use Birkman reports for team building.

• Compaq Computer has used Birkman materials for courses in stress management.

• Ford Motor Corporation relied on Birkman's expertise to assist in its organizational restructuring during the 1980s and continues to use Birkman reports for senior management development consulting work.

• William M. Mercer, Inc., the largest benefits consultancy in the world, uses Birkman for personal/executive development and as part of a supervisory skills training program.

• Electrical and natural gas utilities (Columbia Gas, Arkla, and Central Power and Light, among others) are Birkman clients, receiving personal and team development training.

- Most of the major oil companies (Tenneco, Amoco, Arco, Exxon, Shell, and others) have made use of Birkman materials for a variety of purposes.

- Gerald Hines Interests, a property management company described by *Fortune* magazine as "the most active real estate developer in America," has been using the Birkman services with property managers for *over thirty-five years*.

In addition to these specific users of the vast scope of Birkman resources, thousands of other clients come to Birkman & Associates, Inc., to receive help in assessment and development, vocational/avocational guidance, interpersonal skills development, selection and placement, stress management and conflict resolution, life planning, team building, sales training, outplacement, and much more.

However, don't think that you need to be in some large corporation with specific business problems to benefit from what Roger Birkman has to share with you. The conceptual building blocks of his whole method are the unique patterns of *perceptions of each individual*. While many people come to him for help with business *applications* of his method, it is just as effective and helpful for any individual trying to cope with the normal, stressful situations of life. Organizations (businesses, churches, and other groups) benefit only as their *members,* both individually and collectively, are helped to see the "bigger picture" of their relationships and interactions with other people.

Whether you're a CEO trying to make your company as strong as possible, a parent who needs to understand his or her kids better, or a person wanting to understand your unique qualities more clearly, this book will give you a clearer perspective of your current situation and what you need to do next. By learning a little bit more about the perceptions that you've always taken for granted, you may be surprised how much of an improvement you will see in your relationships, your peace of mind, your level of hope, and your overall outlook on life.

—The Publishers

PREFACE

For as long as I can remember, I have been fascinated by the topic of perception. When we perceive things correctly and make valid assumptions based on our perceptions, we can be optimistic and hopeful. Yet all too often something happens to distort our perception. We fail to see things clearly, or we see correctly yet fail to come to the right conclusions based on what we have seen. When we know what to do, it's not too difficult to deal with the problem and get back on track. Yet few of us know how to restore clear vision after our perceptions have become distorted.

The power of perception became very evident to me during World War II. As a B-17 bomber pilot, I witnessed times when my fellow pilots, under great stress, wasted valuable ammunition on targets they perceived to be there (but actually were not). Since then, I have tried to identify, analyze, and learn how to eliminate many other types of perception problems.

For example, why do some of the nicest people go through life being perceived as harsh or uncaring? And is there anything that can be done to help them deal with the misperceptions other people have about them?

And how about *you?* Do you always behave consistently? If not, why not? Any inconsistency on your part can quickly become a perception problem for the people who regularly interact with you.

I became so intrigued with such issues that I started a company,

Birkman & Associates, Inc., to explore this phenomenon and discover the root of the problem. And what I've discovered in the past forty-plus years is that the problem is not really much of a problem at all. People's behavior usually makes perfectly good sense. Almost always, people act the way they do for a good reason. And they behave consistently, *depending upon their current state of mind.*

You see, most people behave one way when they are relaxed and "being themselves." They act another way when experiencing stress. But in both cases they are behaving consistently. It is possible to observe a person's actions and determine whether or not he or she is currently stressed out. And when you identify the condition, you will know how to respond to the person in a way that will be most helpful. The purpose of this book is not so much to produce change (in you and those around you) or to criticize behaviors. In terms of personality, there are no determinations of good or bad, right or wrong. Rather, my single goal for this book is *to help you understand why people act as they do.* And the simple ability to understand will provide untold insights into your personal relationships, interactions at work, and, best of all, into understanding why *you* do the things you do.

In fact, though my business is usually considered one of "consulting," I try to act instead as an "information-provider" for our clients. I have no desire to be perceived as the "expert" who imparts answers to others. Rather, I prefer to operate in partnership with the client. He or she is always the expert when it comes to that particular organization. But if I can provide enough information, that person should be able to see more clearly his or her options and eventual solutions. My desire is to help people "manage their perceptions."

I have tried to use the same approach in this book. You won't find a list of "Things to Do Differently." Instead, you will find a few of the things I've discovered during my life's study of human behavior and will be able to apply the information to your own specific situation. As a note of preparation, you will see the term *consultant(s)* used throughout the book. I have intentionally tried to keep the staff of my company small enough to be manageable. I like to be personally involved with each of the clients who come to our headquarters in Houston for help or advice. Yet, in order to accommodate more people, we enlist the services of professional business consultants throughout the country. So when I refer to "our consultants," I mean those independent consultants who use The Birkman Method in their work. These people have been brought into our headquarters and taught the intricacies of our assessment method.

The reality of life is that your perceptions—right or wrong—influence everything else you do. When you get a proper perspective on your perceptions, you may be surprised how many other things fall into place. I hope this book is the beginning of a wonderful transformation for you.

—Roger Birkman

CHAPTER 1

IF AT FIRST YOU DON'T PERCEIVE . . .

Suppose you are walking down the street and notice that a crowd has gathered around a teenager. A sign in front of him reads: "The Amazing Wesley." An adult, standing nearby, encourages people to shout out any two numbers and tells them that Wesley will multiply the numbers immediately. One person yells out, "Twenty-three times seventeen." Without a moment's hesitation, Wesley fires back, "Three hundred ninety-one."

Another person suggests, "Eight hundred forty-three times thirty-three." Again the answer comes immediately: "Twenty-seven thousand, eight hundred nineteen."

Since you figure it would be easy to prearrange certain numbers with "plants" in the audience, *you* yell out, "How about 4,666 times 8,459?" And before you can even think, *Let's see him do* that *one,* his young voice replies, "Thirty-nine million, four hundred sixty-nine thousand, six hundred ninety-four." Of course, it takes you an embarrassingly long time to pull out a pen and paper to verify that he is absolutely correct. You are awestruck to be in the presence of such a genius.

As you move on down the street, you see that another crowd has formed around a young girl named Kelly. She stands beside a piano as members of the audience are invited to step up and play a piece of music. When they finish, you are told that she will repeat the exact piece they have played—note for note, including their mistakes.

One person plays part of Bach's "Brandenburg Concerto No. 3." A second plays portions of Elton John's "Rocket Man." A third plays something no one recognizes—perhaps a personal improvisation. No matter. As each person finishes, Kelly performs an exact duplication of the song, as accurately as if it were being replayed on a tape recorder.

As you continue to walk, you discover that you have stumbled upon some kind of exhibition. You find many other people with amazing skills and abilities. One can provide the square root or cube root of any number. One can write any word or sentence upside down and backwards—without pausing to think about what he is doing. Another observes as a handful of peas is tossed onto a tabletop, and instantly gives the correct number.

Since it quickly becomes obvious to you that none of these demonstrations is rigged, you begin to feel a little uncomfortable in the presence of so many people who appear to be among the brightest in the world. You feel a bit intimidated or ashamed of your own "shortcomings." Maybe even downright envious. If you happened to be with your kids, you might even chide, "Now why can't *you* do that?"

At home, dwelling on your inadequacies, you might even be tempted to hire a private tutor to bring you and your family "up to speed" in math, music, and other areas. But if you had stuck around a while longer, you would have noticed that the demonstrations you had just witnessed were examples of "savant syndrome." (In the movie *Rain Man,* the character portrayed by Dustin Hoffman was severely retarded but able to function with brilliance in the area of mathematics.)

In real life, there have been people like the Amazing Wesley who could multiply with great precision, yet as a cashier would be unable to make change for a dollar. People like Kelly have been noted for their precise musical imitation, yet were otherwise retarded and unable to care for themselves. In September 1993, the London *Times* reported on a nineteen-year-old British youth whose musical ability was being compared to Mozart. Possessing perfect pitch, he could "hold" music in his head, playing it mentally and hearing exactly how it would sound. In addition, with one glance at a building, he could draw it with amazing accuracy and perspective. Otherwise, the young man was described as, "withdrawn, mute . . . of apparently low intelligence."

My interest as a psychologist is not in the area of savant syndrome and what makes those people so different from the rest of the world. I am, however, fascinated by what such people represent in terms of how we tend to perceive others.

For example, if you had witnessed only the particular ability of the people described previously, you might make certain assumptions:

- "I'm in the presence of genius."

- "I wish I could do what that person can do."

- "He/she is much more intelligent than I could ever be."

- "If my teachers had done a better job, I could probably do that too."

- "If I could do what he could do, I'd be rich!"

These assumptions, while entirely accurate, are quite incomplete. Now you know that your assumptions were based on one—but only one—element of the person's character and abilities.

The same is true in life: You see it with your own eyes. You fully know and believe it to be true. And you begin to form opinions (and in some cases, even decisions) based on what you have seen.

But the problem here lies in what you *don't* see. We tend to fill in unknown facts about other people with characteristics we know to be true about ourselves. For example, based on what you have seen, you might assume that the Amazing Wesley is destined to be a straight-A student, president of the National Honor Society, class valedictorian, college-bound, and able to name his job and salary. You might never suspect that he will spend his life tended by caretakers who must see that no harm comes to him because of his inability to do the simplest chores on his own. Your perception was accurate. Your assumptions, however, are far off target.

The reverse is true as well. If you observed the person's usual state of helplessness, you would be likely to make certain assumptions based on *that* perception. And you would be just as flabbergasted to suddenly find that person solving "impossible" math problems or performing incredible musical feats.

One major goal of this book will be to help identify similar (though obviously less severe) contrasts as we deal with "normal" people— parents, children, bosses, friends. We often make assumptions about the people in our lives based on our perceptions of them. In many cases, our perceptions may be correct. Our assumptions, however, may be off-target for several reasons:

- We may misinterpret the behaviors of the person.

- The person may act one way while thinking and feeling another.

- Our perceptions may be limited to one particular aspect of the person (business, family, church) with no knowledge of other roles.

- We may project our own emotions and/or attitudes onto the other person's behaviors.

What Is Perception?

For purposes of this book, the dictionary definition I like best is: *Perception* is "a mental image." I will write in terms of perceptions (plural) rather than one's overall perception (impression) about something. Most of the time our perceptions are neutral. We see, hear, or sense something, and make a mental note of the perception. For example:

- John didn't laugh at my joke about the guy getting fired.

- Betsy's math grade dropped from straight A's to a C.

- I didn't enjoy that movie as much as the rest of the group seemed to.

- My wife always does better than I do when we're watching *Jeopardy.*

- My boss jokes around a lot with other staff members, but is serious with me most of the time.

In each of these examples, the perception is like a mental snapshot that gets filed away in the memory. And, like a photo album, the collection of pictures may reflect an accurate rendering as seen through the lens of the camera.

However, the *assumptions* one makes in response to perceptions may or may not be correct. Some may be positive and others may be negative. Perceptions, therefore, while usually accurate and neutral, tend to spawn certain assumptions that may be inaccurate and biased.

Right Perceptions, Right Assumptions

Perhaps at some point in your life it has been necessary to check your blood pressure, cholesterol, temperature, or some other physical function at regular intervals. If so, you have probably learned the importance of taking a *series* of readings. A single, isolated number doesn't do much good unless you know what is "normal" for you.

Perceptions work in much the same way. As you accumulate them over months or years, you learn to identify which ones may be abnormal. Then, as you make assumptions based on your perceptions, you can do so with a significant amount of confidence. Watch a couple who has been married for many years. They get to a point where they can communicate almost effortlessly. A brief perception of the other person's body language, tone of voice, facial expression, or mood can lead to instant assumptions that the person is happy, sad, confused, or angry. Yet this is possible only because of the thousands of "readings" that have been taken over the years and the information they have gleaned from each other. The spouse is not making assumptions based on an isolated perception, but rather on how that particular perception compares with the accumulated data gathered from all the previous perceptions of their history together. Because of the time spent together and the privilege of having seen the other person in the widest possible variety of settings and emotional states, the spouse can make accurate assumptions based on his or her perceptions.

However, very few relationships allow such a complete and detailed reading of one's perceptions. Even the parent/child relationship is sometimes difficult to read. A parent can have unconditional love for the child, but the child's needs are continually changing. During the early growth stages, the child needs nurturing and protection, then independence and self-identity, and later, mentoring and parental examples. The parents' "database" of perceptions cannot be stabilized for years. If they assume a nurturing role while the child is seeking independence, they can make wrong assumptions about what the child wants or needs. If they stand back and try to let the child grapple with independence when she really wants affirmation and hugs, they won't understand her frustration. Later in life, after the child has discovered his or her own unique strengths and personality traits, the parent/child ability to correctly "read" each other becomes a bit simpler.

And in relationships where the readings of the other person are few and far apart, the assumptions we make on our perceptions can be drastically inaccurate.

Right Perceptions, Wrong Assumptions

Do you remember the story of the blind men and the elephant? Five blind men, who had never seen an elephant and had no prior knowledge of them, were allowed to interact with a live elephant. The first one reached out and happened to grasp one of the elephant's tusks. *Oh, so that's it,* he thought. *An elephant is thin and hard, like a spear.*

The second man, standing right beside the first, discovered the elephant's trunk. His perception was that an elephant must be long and flexible, not unlike a large snake.

The third blind man, not two steps away from the others, came upon the elephant's ear. *What a wonderful animal,* he thought, *to be light and airy, like a large fan.*

The fourth man, a bit shorter than the others, stepped forward and happened to get his arms around one of the elephant's massive legs. He came to the very logical conclusion that an elephant was very much like a tree.

The last man, approaching from a different direction, found the elephant's tail. His assumption was that the elephant was like a rope. It was even a bit frayed at the end that he held.

As the five blind men left and began their journey home, they began to discuss their perceptions. Each could hardly believe how dense the others were for not coming to the "correct" conclusion. None of them were ever able to convince the others that he was right and they were wrong. And none of them would concede that the others might be right—not after what each one had just experienced firsthand!

So who was right? They all were! Each of the five men had an absolutely correct, firsthand perception of an elephant. The problem was that each man had only *one* perception. And with such a limited perspective (on so large a matter as an elephant), it was impossible for them to reach a mutually satisfactory conclusion.

We make the same, or at least similar, mistakes when we make assumptions based on a limited number of perceptions. Dealing daily with massive issues such as love, religion, business, school, marriage, self-image, depression, relationships—the "elephants" in our lives— we have a number of perceptions on file concerning each subject. But very likely we have not accumulated enough information to form an accurate view of the whole issue.

Few of us would venture to buy a new home based on the picture and price in the real estate agent's book. A picture simply doesn't tell us all we need to know. We'd want to see the house for ourselves. What does the surrounding neighborhood look like? Is the foundation solid? Are there any signs of previous flood or fire? Does the interior measure up to the exterior? We'd want to deal with these and dozens of other issues before making a decision to buy or not to buy.

Similarly, we need a number of accurate perceptions before we make any assumptions about ourselves, our loved ones, our coworkers, or the world around us. Remember that a perception is a mental image—a mental snapshot, so to speak. A close-up of an elephant's tusk, trunk, ear, leg, or tail would not help us much in knowing what an elephant looked like. But if we had all five images and believed that they were all accurate, we could begin to get a realistic picture. Better still, we might decide to back off from the elephant far enough to get a picture of the entire animal—or at least the side facing the camera. We might even want to get pictures from several different angles. Then, with our collection of snapshots (perceptions), we could begin to understand how all the various pieces are part of the greater whole.

If you met me for the first time, you would have certain perceptions about me. I hope you would think I was a kind and considerate person, knowledgeable about my work and professional concerns. But I doubt that you could make accurate assumptions about my whole personality. You probably wouldn't know that I used to be a B-17 bomber pilot. You probably never have seen me play tennis. You wouldn't know what kind of relationship I have with my wife and family. You wouldn't know whether or not I leave my socks lying around the house for my wife to pick up. You might make assumptions about these kinds of things, but those assumptions would be based more on what you know about yourself than on what you know about me. (This concept will be developed more fully in later chapters.)

Though your perceptions about me could be entirely accurate, several factors might prevent you from being able to make the correct assumptions. For one thing, you simply wouldn't have enough "snapshots" to get a complete picture. You would need to observe me over a long period of time, in a variety of settings, before you could tell whether your initial readings of me were accurate.

Another complicating factor would be the fact that, if we were just introduced, I would be likely to be on my best behavior—"role play-ing," so to speak. I have trained myself to "perform" a certain way in social settings that may or may not reflect my true nature. For example, I am something of an introvert. However, you might read me as talkative, self-assured, and professional. You couldn't tell how I respond in an informal setting around people who know me well. (In most cases, only good friends feel entirely comfortable spending long periods of time with each other without feeling the necessity of keeping a conversation going.)

It is in the area of making wrong assumptions based on correct perceptions where this book will focus. When we are too quick to jump to conclusions, or when we make key assumptions based on limited information, our misassumptions can lead to serious confusion or emotional damage. Making right assumptions based on right per-ceptions is never a problem. And only a small percentage of people get to the point where their perspective is so distorted that they develop warped perceptions. But a great many of us are guilty of forming misassumptions even though we have perceived correctly.

Wrong Perceptions, Wrong Assumptions

While our perceptions are *usually* accurate, they can sometimes become distorted over a period of time. This is especially true when it comes to self-perceptions. When children are never affirmed or encouraged, they begin to see themselves through the eyes of their uncaring parents, so they never develop a sense of value or self-worth. Later in life, they may be confronted with the truth that *everyone* has unique strengths and abilities. But in some cases, no amount of evidence will cause them to change their minds about themselves. Over time, the overpowering opinions of others have eventually caused them to lose the ability to perceive themselves (and conse-quently, other people) accurately. Even when they try their hardest to believe the evidence that is presented to them, they find it next to impossible to trust those perceptions.

To illustrate, take a look at the following optical illusions:

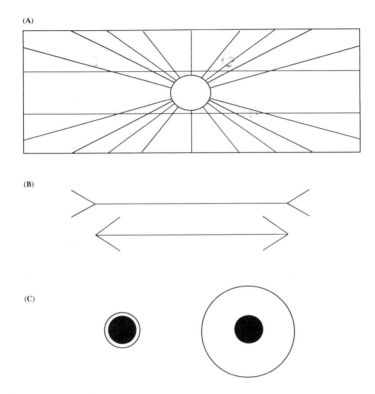

Are the bold lines in Illusion A bowed in the middle? In Illusion B, is line A-B longer than line B-C? In Illusion C, is the second center dot larger than the first one? In each case, you would think so. Yet believe it or not, the lines are parallel, A-B is the same length as B-C, and the center circles are the same size. Optical illusions force our eyes to make misperceptions. And just as your eye can be tricked to perceive things inaccurately, your emotions can be similarly manipu-lated to misperceive certain situations. When this happens, it usually takes some professional help for the person to eventually regain confidence in his or her perceptions.

Wrong Perceptions, Right Assumptions

In rare instances, we may struggle to reconcile what we *know* to be true (on a cognitive level) with what we *perceive* (incorrectly) to be true. For example, a person who receives no affirmation as a child may not perceive himself to be of any value, yet can be convinced, intellectually, that he is. But it is little consolation for a person who doesn't *feel* worthwhile to *think* that he is. Until his perceptions match his intellectual beliefs, the person is in for a period of emotional turmoil. In most such cases, the cognitive beliefs will change before the perceptions do.

Our perceptions are powerful. When you look at a photograph, you instinctively believe that what you're seeing is exactly what the camera saw. But maybe the camera was set at the wrong f-stop, or the picture was taken through a fish-eye lens, distorting certain parts. Maybe a problem in the development of the picture caused the colors to fade or appear unreal. The only way to be sure is to check the picture against the actual scene where it was taken.

When we analyze our perceptions, we assume them to be accurate. But distortions do occasionally creep in, and they are hard to identify. The important step to take in such instances is to deal with the misperceptions until you can get your life back in proper focus again. Investigate to see whether or not something is distorting your perceptions—the basis of your relationships, self-worth, decisions, etc. This book will help ensure that your perceptions are accurate. Distortions are nothing to be feared. They are far more threatening and painful when ignored than when faced head-on.

Goal(s) of This Book

As we examine this area of perception together, you will find out how to identify and maximize your strengths while learning ways to compensate for any weaknesses. You'll see how other people think and operate, and as you discover the differences, you may begin to understand those "strange" people for the first time. You'll examine your own perceptions and make sure that you are seeing clearly, enabling you to make good decisions and create strong and healthy relationships. You'll learn how to strengthen the relationships that mean most to you—coworkers, family members, friends—and most importantly, you'll come to understand yourself.

Back in 1597 Francis Bacon wrote: "Knowledge is power." In this day of emotional chaos and personal confusion, the better we know ourselves, the stronger our character and confidence. It is my hope that you will come to know yourself through the pages of this book and will be enabled to face life with poise and serenity.

CHAPTER 2

WATCH HOW YOU ACT!

Before reading this chapter, take the following pop quiz. Answer True or False, depending upon whether or not you have ever performed the activity described. (True = Yes, I've done this; False = No, never!)

Attempted to impress a member of the opposite sex by appearing smarter or more talented than I actually am.

Exaggerated a resumé to appear more qualified than I really am.

Tried to persuade someone to buy something or do something using a method I learned in a book or manual.

"Said grace" over a meal while hosting visitors, when I don't normally make a habit of doing so.

Imitated a particular behavior I saw and liked in another person.

"Put on a happy face" when, in fact, I felt lousy.

If you checked more "True" boxes than "False," this chapter is for you! From this simple test, you can easily see how others might tend to perceive your behaviors and come to an erroneous conclusion. And while you're trying to guarantee that other people think the best about you, you can be sure they're doing the same kinds of things to make a good impression too.

From the time we were small children, most of us were trained to act in ways that are quite unnatural. Of course, most of our parents tried to teach us good manners and etiquette: "Keep your elbows off the table. Don't talk with food in your mouth. Cover your mouth when you sneeze."

But the training soon extended beyond basic rules of behavior:

- "We're having Daddy's boss for dinner, so don't you dare repeat any of those bad jokes you've heard us telling."

- "When you shake hands with someone you meet, press firmly so you'll appear confident."

- "I know you call your sister that name, but you'd better not let your teacher at school hear you!"

Socialized Behavior

We quickly learn that there is one set of behaviors that we can use in the comfort and privacy of our homes, though some of us may receive mixed messages from parents as well: "Children should be seen and not heard." But the rules change when we get out into the world: "Here's how to succeed in school, business, and life." Parents pass along the secrets of getting along with teachers and bosses—most of which have little to do with being oneself. From childhood we begin to absorb the nuances of "socially acceptable behavior." Sometimes we wrap so many layers of such behaviors around the core of our personalities that we find it hard to distinguish who we really are. At my company we use the term *socialized* behavior to refer to the actions people take to be perceived as socially acceptable. Such actions may or may not reflect the reality of their own personalities. And, with practice, some of us become so adept at using our socialized behaviors that they appear to be quite natural.

I know of a noted author who has written a number of books that have struck deep chords with the reading public. Almost before he knew it, he was being asked to speak to large audiences across the country. The people wanted to get to know the man behind the message. Having had a great deal of training in public speaking, the author was well received. But at one of his speaking engagements, he surprised a lot of people by confessing how much of an introvert he was. Because he could hold everyone's attention, the widespread assumption was that he was a real "people person." But he didn't really enjoy the spotlight. He much preferred to be alone, at home, working on the books that had attracted people to him in the first place.

The man's socialized behavior was well developed. He could stand in front of a crowd and appear to be an outgoing, dynamic character. But that wasn't the real person. His outgoing demeanor had nothing to do with his personal needs or interests. Yet because he was such an effective speaker, many listeners had made incorrect assumptions about him.

How about you? To what extent do you use socialized behavior out of necessity—just to get by in the world? To what extent do you use it out of choice—because you don't want people to see you as you really are, or because you want to impress them?

I don't suggest that socialized behavior is wrong. In fact, it is sometimes necessary. If all of us remained true to our personal natures and characters, some of us would rarely ever go out in public. Others would seldom stop talking. But we learn what is socially acceptable and what is expected, and we adapt to those codes as we interact with others. Therefore, my challenge to you is to learn how to differentiate between your socialized behaviors and the behavior that stems from your true self.

During my career as a business consultant, I have dealt with thousands of people who were miserable in their jobs. Why would they take a job they detested? In most cases, it is because they mastered the socialized behavior necessary to get the job. But once they were hired, they were afraid to admit that they had not presented themselves completely truthfully.

In thousands of books, there are secrets, steps, formulas, acronyms, and other tips to help the reader succeed in one way or another. Authors will show you how to write a resumé, how to conduct yourself in a job interview, how to influence people, how to make the sale, how to get rich quick, how to dress for success, and on and on. But few of these books recommend just being yourself. They usually advise adopting some degree of socialized behavior, which in some cases is little more than "acting." And these books are of little value once the person lands the job and discovers, too late, that it is not tailored to his personality or strengths.

Through the years your parents, teachers, bosses, spouse, and many others have subtly or not so subtly tried to show you how to act in certain situations. Books and magazines provide advice on getting ahead in the world. Television and movies portray characters who lead self-actualized lives and are rewarded for it, or those who don't and must suffer the consequences. If you're like most people, you've picked up bits and pieces of your behavior from all these sources. Perhaps, as a result, you're a well-rounded person. On the other hand, maybe you're just confused!

Fear of Self-Discovery

In my work, when promising to help people identify their strengths and weaknesses, I encounter frequent resistance. Some people who have become successful at "hiding behind" socialized behavior are reluctant to consider the truth about who they really are. Most people don't mind dealing with their strengths, but prefer to close their eyes to any possible weaknesses.

Though this is a fairly common reaction, I find it a bit unsettling. The world needs introverts as well as extroverts. We need people who love to deal with numbers as well as those who love to deal with people. We need dancers, firemen, plumbers, bankers, salespeople, computer programmers, musicians, and a full array of vocational variety. No one person is capable of doing everything equally well. All of us are stronger in some areas than in others.

Similarly, no one is equally qualified to perform all the duties of any single job. Any business requires a wide variety of skills: accounting, research and development, packaging, marketing, design, sales, customer service, and so forth. It should not be threatening to try to discover which functions you are best suited for and which should be on the bottom of your list. But for some people, this is an ordeal.

I know of some who have stayed in jobs they detested—bored to death, burned out, and with no hope of advancement—simply because they were fearful of finding out they might be better qualified to do something else. I have learned a great deal from such people. For whatever their reasons, I understand their reluctance to risk change.

When we conduct personal or professional evaluations, my company strives to focus on the positive aspects of an employee—his or her strengths. Yet it is only possible to view strengths in the context of the things the person dislikes or doesn't do as well. I cannot overemphasize: *A person's "weaknesses" are never a negative indication*. Weaknesses simply point us to our strengths. And the sooner we discover which aspects of any job we are best suited for, the sooner we can begin to figure out why we feel the way we do about ourselves, our jobs, and other people.

I must be honest and confess that I only recently learned to "practice what I preach." For many of the forty years Birkman & Associates, Inc. has been in business, I felt we needed to publish books to let people know what we have learned from our research, what we believe about perception and personality, and what services we can provide. But I never felt qualified to sit down and write a book.

While speaking with a business friend in the Houston area recently, I admitted to being a bit envious of his company's wide range of publications. "Roger," he said, "don't you know? We get help!" He went on to tell me about people who are skilled in producing publishable manuscripts from random ideas, stacks of unrelated materials, and seminars on cassette. While I had certainly spoken enough to produce any number of books, I needed help in weeding through my ideas and organizing them. In the meantime, I could devote my time and energy to doing the things I was more qualified to do.

The result of our concerted efforts is this book. What I hope it will do is to open your eyes to some of your weaker areas and, thus, to your greatest strengths. Only when you begin to deal with those basic perceptions will you be able to understand your true self and find your proper "fit" in life.

The poet e.e. cummings wrote: "it takes courage to grow up and turn out to be who you really are." I could do no greater service than to help you discover "who you really are." Until you can separate your socialized behavior from your genuine personality, others will relate to you *as they perceive you*. The more you demonstrate socialized behavior that doesn't reflect who you are, the harder it will be for others to know the real you.

I know of another speaker and author who is noted for his sense of humor and seemingly unlimited optimism. He is the life of every convention where he appears, and people crowd around him at every opportunity, hanging on every word. They admire his compassion, his wonderful humanity, and his ability to make others laugh and feel better about themselves.

In recent years, however, this man has suffered a great deal of physical pain and family problems. Since he isn't yet ready to share these heavy burdens with the public, he is forced to carry on as if nothing has happened. As he packs up to go to speaking engagements where he will address such issues as motivation, overcoming stress, and strengthening interpersonal relationships, it is sometimes all he can do to quell his own depression. Yet when he arrives, he "acts" the part he is expected to play. His socialized behavior takes over, and he continues to influence people.

It seems a pity that few, if any, of his listeners will ever relate to this man in a way that will be meaningful to *him*. But until he is ready to reveal his true feelings and become vulnerable to his audiences, he will continue to suffer. Of course, it is somewhat understandable in his case—his whole life revolves around his work. Yet I suspect that even more people would be able to relate to his pain and suffering than to his collection of jokes, amusing anecdotes, and motivational phrases.

This man may be stuck in the rut of his socialized behavior, but what about you? It takes courage to open up to others. Change always involves some degree of risk: What if you finally allow others to see the real you and they don't like what they see? On the other hand, what if when you begin to open up to other people, they like you even better and jump at the opportunity to share themselves with you as well? The world is waiting for a few courageous pioneers to get the ball rolling.

The potential of expanding the scale of intimacy is exciting. Most of us have one or two close friends to whom we can confide some of our inner feelings. As people begin to be willing to discover who they really are and share that information with others (family, business associates, etc.), unexpected and wonderful things can happen.

The "big mouth" suddenly sees what makes the "shrinking violet" the way she is. The accounting people realize that the marketing people don't dislike them, they just see things differently. The editorial people stop criticizing the sales brochures and are asked to help write them. And in return, the next time one of those introverted editors is supposed to make a presentation, the sales people can give tips on how to make it go smoothly.

Smart business managers recognize the importance of trying to get past the socialized behaviors of their employees. In spite of the expense, they send their executives off on rafting trips, sponsor company picnics and other get-togethers, and schedule important planning meetings away from the usual corporate setting. Since people get so good at socialized behavior in one arena, a change of locale sometimes helps them "lower their guard." And when employees see each other in casual clothes, for example, with defenses down, communication begins to improve and innate personality has the opportunity to overcome image.

Many churches, too, realize the importance of retreats. In fact, church is one of the places where socialized behavior is practiced most rigorously. From the time many of us are small children, we're told how to behave in church. (And for most of us, it isn't at all like our "usual" behavior.) Yet in the woods or some other natural setting, worship takes on a whole new dimension.

Whenever we're overly concerned with acting as we *should* rather than behaving as we *are,* we will experience inner dissonance. Sometimes we even lose the ability to differentiate between our real selves and the facade we've created for others. But there is hope, even for those most deeply entrenched in socialized behavior.

As you continue to work through the rest of this book, challenge yourself to be completely honest. Try to get in touch with how you really feel. The need for socialized behavior won't disappear entirely. You may still have to go to work every morning wearing a business suit, a smile, and a steely look in your eye. But remember that underneath that suit and behind that smile is the real you, with firm beliefs and confidence in your own unique strengths. It can make a remarkable difference!

CHAPTER 3

YOU AREN'T NORMAL

The story is told of a trapper who occasionally loaded up his donkey with furs and sold them at a large city about a half-day's journey from his home. Deciding one day that his young son was old enough to accompany him, the man set out on foot, the boy walking along beside him. Since it was a pleasant day, neither of them minded.

On the way home that evening, they continued to walk, even though the donkey was no longer carrying his heavy load. As they passed through a village, they heard the townspeople mocking them: "What fools! Leading a beast of burden while they both walk! In our village, we would have the good sense to ride!" The father thought, *They may be right. The boy could probably use a rest.* So he placed his son on the back of the donkey and continued on his way.

In the next town more villagers gathered as they passed by. "What has this world come to?" they called out. "A fine strapping young lad rides while his poor father is forced to walk. Why, in our village, young people have respect for their elders." The man listened and came to another conclusion. *They may be right. Perhaps I should trade places with my son.* So he did.

As they entered the next town, it didn't take the father long to hear other comments: "How sad. Look at the selfish father who rides his donkey while his young son straggles behind. In our village this man would be reported to the proper authorities and the poor boy placed in a good home." The father was instantly contrite. *They may be right. What was I thinking?* So this time he got onto the donkey with his son.

As father and son rode into the next village, the people were outraged. "What cruel mistreatment of a fine animal! In our village, that man and his son would be put into the stocks for making a defenseless animal carry all that weight. And we would show proper respect by carrying the donkey." The man thought the idea highly unusual, but to appease all the onlookers, he did what they had suggested. He and his son dismounted, and struggling beneath the weight of the donkey, they lifted the confused animal onto their shoulders and carried it out of town.

When they entered the next village, no one said a word. The man assumed that their silence meant he had finally discovered how to please people. In reality, the townspeople simply thought it inappropriate to make fun of fools!

This story might be laughable except that the same thing takes place every day in thousands of businesses and even families—good people trying their very best to satisfy everyone else. But what it takes to make one person happy may be completely different from what is required by another person. If you've ever been in charge of a project, you probably know the frustration of trying to get approval from various divisions. You may have no trouble getting support for your brilliant idea from your immediate boss. But then you must travel through the "villages" of marketing, accounting, research and development, ad infinitum. And in trying to please all of them, you may end up carrying a donkey!

Or you might learn what pleases one boss only to have him or her leave and be replaced by another whose operating style is completely different. At times, even the same person can seemingly expect one thing one day and something else the next. The special treat you had for your kids last week may be "old hat" by this week. And before long you start to ask yourself: What's wrong with all these people? Or is something wrong with *me?* What's *normal* in these situations?

Six Common Myths

Wouldn't it be nice to have some kind of business or interpersonal "thermometer" you could use to determine how far off 98.6 any situation is? As hard as some people try to devise such methods to separate what's "normal" from what isn't, it can't be done. But we *can* better understand our families, our companies, and other group interactions by becoming aware of several deceptive myths. As you begin to see past these six common myths and get to the truth, your relationships on the job (or in other settings) should begin to make a lot more sense.

Myth #1: I'm normal, and anyone who is different from me is not normal.

We have referred to the assumptions we make, and how sometimes we find ourselves in trouble because we assume incorrectly. Perhaps nowhere is this problem more acute than in the instances where managers, parents, or other leaders assume that one particular set of criteria is "normal" while all others deviate from that singular norm.

What determines what is "normal" by our own inner definitions? Usually we base our opinions on our own characteristics:

- Look how much time he needs to make a decision! He's not executive material!

- Can't he see that this is a pin-stripe company? Why does he insist on those Oxford tweeds?

- If Sarah doesn't play up to the boss more often, she's never going to get promoted.

As we observe people and situations around us, we may automatically determine to what extent they are behaving "normally," based on our instinctive definitions. Meanwhile, those people are looking back at us and wondering why *we* are so strange! How can we be so casual in decision-making, so stuffy in dress, and so servile in our attitudes toward upper management? We may seem quite abnormal to them. So who is right?

If I may borrow President Coolidge's definition, normalcy is never a matter of "us" or "them." If my years of study in the field of psychology have taught me anything, it's that no set of criteria exists anywhere to help us define "normal." Therefore, nobody is normal. And everyone is.

We probably have characteristics and interests in common with many other individuals, yet we cannot assume that anyone who doesn't share those characteristics is not normal. Once we institute standards of what is normal, whether formal or implied, we impede the ability of other people to get a job done. This leads to the next myth.

Myth #2: My way is the best way.

We learn from experience, but our experience is usually based on our unique interests, needs, and personal strengths. Consequently, the methods you devise may seem awkward and unnatural to me. And my way of doing things may not work at all for you.

Yet how many times do you or others try to accomplish a goal in exactly the same manner as someone else? Thousands, or perhaps millions, of books and tapes are sold every year touting "Five Secrets to Successful Selling" or "Seven Steps to Fame and Riches." "It worked for me," promises the author. But even if it is an honest claim, the same steps may not work for every single person who tries them. If every individual is unique in his or her strengths and abilities, how can we expect one standard of behavior to work equally well for all?

Perhaps a larger problem is the imposition of our own expectations on other people. Whether we are dealing with our children or our employees, many of us are unable to lay out an assignment or task without also laying out the specific steps to take in order to get the job done. We believe this myth. We are convinced that "My way is the best way."

Only by truly valuing another's uniqueness will we be able to steer that person toward a task and then allow him or her to accomplish it in his own way. We may be quite surprised to discover how many "right" ways there are of doing something—none of which may be "my" way.

Myth #3: The way a person acts is the way he or she needs to be treated.

Sometimes people defy logic or reason in their actions and attitudes. For example, perhaps you know a straightforward, no-nonsense go-getter who always speaks with laconic authority. Those who deal with him know better than to question his judgment; they simply listen to his directions and comply with his wishes.

If you wanted to communicate with this person, how would you do it? Your natural tendency might be to keep all communication short and to the point. After all, it certainly seems to be the style this person prefers. But again, *this is an assumption based on perception.* Just because a person acts boldly and aggressively doesn't necessarily mean that he or she wants to be treated in a similar style.

When people take personality evaluations, it is not at all unusual to discover an *active behavior* at one end of the scale and a *personal need* at the other. So your brash, curt, and outspoken coworker may need to have things expressed to him slowly and patiently. We cannot always tell by observing someone's behavior how he or she actually prefers to be treated.

If you're honest with yourself, you can probably see the fallacy of this myth based on some of your own actions. Maybe you're good at detaching your feelings from business interactions and decisions. Some managers intentionally try not to get too involved in the everyday lives of the people who report to them, citing the need to remain objective and unbiased. Yet those same people may desire a warm and personal relationship with their own supervisors. Or maybe you prefer structure so you know exactly where you stand in a company, yet you provide freedom for the people who report to you. But the fact remains that you cannot tell from a person's outward behavior how that person *needs* to be treated.

Myth #4: Most people feel the way I do.

What is true about outward behavior is also true of inner feelings. The natural, human tendency of most people is to fill in unknown characteristics about others from what they know about themselves. Suppose you come to work for my company, and in a meeting I disagree with something you've said. I don't know you very well, and if I have a natural aversion to direct confrontation, I may assume the same thing about you. As a result, you may not find out what I'm really thinking unless you read some of my subtle signals. Yet you may thrive on blunt disagreement and debate. I would, therefore, be missing a good opportunity for clear communication by assuming that you feel the same way I do in the area of confrontation.

In most cases, it is absolutely right for you to feel as you do. It is also right for other people to feel as *they* do. We need to learn to communicate our preferences to other people and to acknowledge differences among us.

Myth #5: There are plenty of "spectators," but it's the "doers" who get the job done.

"Doers" have lots of names—go-getters, type-A people, extroverts. They usually appear to be the most productive members of a company or group. They are usually quicker to receive recognition, raises, and promotions than the dull, sluggish, seemingly slow-witted people who hardly speak to each other, much less speak up in meetings.

Since "doers" stand out in a crowd, they are easily noticed. But it is a gross injustice to buy into the myth that these are the *only* productive people in the group. Can you envision a world where *everyone* acts the same? I hope not. People who act instinctively and individually are vital, sure, but they depend more than they know on other people.

How about the people in accounting who seem to be more comfortable with numbers than with people, but who can save the company thousands upon thousands of dollars by interpreting their charts, graphs, and percentages? They can analyze exactly how effective the "doers" are. They can separate the ones who are truly successful from those who are generating only smoke and noise.

How about the quietly quirky creative people in the group? In most cases, these are the ones who see the big picture, who steer everyone else toward a well developed business plan. It's great to have a group of people "getting the job done"—as long as they're working toward the same goals. But if they're going in different directions, making decisions and promises based on whims or best guesses, the company may not be able to back up their claims.

And how about the people who support the "doers" with their talent for persuasion? They may have to "sell" people on the decisions and actions being taken by the go-getters—both internally and outside the company. In many cases the "doers" lack sensitivity and tact, assuming that the rest of the world will conform to their way of thinking. That's where the people-oriented individuals come to the rescue.

So can we honestly say that the more aggressive, outspoken "doers" are really more valuable to a company or group than anyone else? Never! They would be completely lost without support from corporate systems (accounting, inventory, shipping, payroll), creative services (planning, advertising, new ideas), and team players (salespeople, teachers, managers). Similarly, individuals in each of these groups depend on the gritty determination of the go-getters in the group.

Consider for a moment how this concept works in a social setting. When you and a group of friends get together, how many of these groupings can you recognize? Perhaps one person is always ready with a suggestion when the rest of the group can't seem to figure out what they want to do. Before the dessert dishes are even picked up, another person has mentally divided out the bill, down to the penny, including tax and tip. Still another person is already planning what to do *next* time you get together. (This is also the person who, after the movie, tells you what the writer and director *should* have done to make it better.) And finally, there are those individuals who truly don't seem to care what the group does, as long as they do it together.

Life would be far less interesting without all of these groupings. Each one provides a valuable service, whether in a social or business setting.

Myth #6: There is one ideal behavioral style.

If you're convinced of the inaccuracies of the previous myths, you should have no problem seeing what's wrong with this one. If no single standard exists for "normal" feelings or behavior, it only makes sense that a wide range of possibilities could be acceptable.

Yet how often do we tend to "write off" certain people, based on a single perception of their behavior? Do any of these comments sound vaguely familiar:

- "She just can't seem to stick to anything. Her mind isn't on her work."

- "I tell him exactly what to do, but he has to do things his own way!"

- "I value her input, but when she's in a meeting, she never says anything. I wonder if she even cares."

- "I stopped asking for his opinion because he always checks with everyone else first, anyway."

As we will see in the next few chapters, some of these problems may not be behavioral "shortcomings" at all. Some people simply take longer to make a good, sound decision. You might see it as a flaw, but another person will view it as a strength. People who aren't good in meetings or in other group settings may provide some of the best ideas if left to themselves for a while. Is this a behavioral weakness? No. It's simply a different personal style.

In chapter 6 we will study a number of components of behavior. The more aware we become of the individual elements that comprise behavior, the better we will be able to understand ourselves. And the better we understand ourselves, the more capable we will be of understanding and relating to others.

You Can Be Dis-Mythed

In my career, one of my primary goals has been to combat the myths that affect so many people. One result of this effort has been the development of my own company's credo. I invite you to examine it, understand it, challenge it if you wish, and create a similar standard for yourself or your own company.

(Please see the credo on the following page.)

These are not just theories or things we hope are true. We prove them true every day as we work with companies and individuals who want to know more about themselves and the people with whom they interact. In the balance of this chapter, I would like to go into a little more detail about each of these beliefs.

Individuals have differences.

The belief that individuals have differences may seem so basic as not to be worth mentioning. Ask anyone and he or she would probably agree on this point. Yet it is possible to believe only on a cognitive level and not put the belief into practice when interacting with others.

Almost as soon as some people begin to discuss various thoughts or behaviors, the conversation quickly shifts to terms of right or wrong, good or bad, their way vs. my way. Therefore, part of understanding that individuals have differences includes resisting the temptation to pass judgment on the behaviors of others.

In acknowledging the differences of individuals, it is important to

WE BELIEVE:

That individuals have differences.

That individuals have both
strengths and weaknesses.

That differences relate to personal,
social, and occupational behavior.

That we should emphasize the
positive aspects of personality.

That individuals can manage
their behavior.

That opportunities for personal
growth should be provided.

try to see that all these ways of relating are right and good and reflect the person's uniqueness, which is the most valuable thing he has to offer to a group. I am not speaking of value systems here, but rather the components of personality. In other words, I feel it is both improper and unwise to polarize our perceptions—for instance, to believe that being outspoken, aggressive, and bold are good or preferable traits, while being shy and introverted is a drawback. People who deal with life through quiet, intense introspection are just as "right" as those who power their way through. And a person who prefers to work alone in a cubicle is no more right or wrong than a person who thrives on group interaction.

Those who are much like ourselves are good. Those who are our diametric opposites are also good. We must learn not only to identify individual differences, but to respect them as well.

Individuals have both strengths and weaknesses.

Only after we struggle to eliminate the right-vs.-wrong mentality should we begin to try to address strengths and weaknesses. From personal experience I am aware of how sensitive people can become when someone even begins to suggest an area of personal weakness. Consequently, our company goes to great lengths to speak in terms of strengths. The very fact that each individual has unique and powerful strengths, however, suggests that other areas will not be as strong.

This is why it is so essential to stop thinking in terms of good/bad and right/wrong. We can't take an honest look at ourselves if we feel threatened or incompetent. Actually, there is great freedom in knowing one's own strengths and weaknesses, for as soon as these are identified, it becomes a much simpler matter to focus on the things you do well and look for help in your weaker areas from *someone who is strong in those areas.*

Life becomes a lot less miserable when you stop doing all the things you detest. Believe it or not, other people *love* to do those tasks you find unbearable. Whether you are in a business or interpersonal setting, you will soon discover that making a few basic trade-offs of responsibility will keep you and the people around you much more cheerful and *productive*. But not before you stand back and take an objective look at yourself—warts and all.

The positive aspects of personality should be emphasized.

Some people find it quite difficult to live with what they perceive to be shortcomings. So if an associate identifies one of their weaknesses, they interpret that as a challenge to "fix it" or "bring it up to speed." For example, one employee may hate dealing with numbers, but will take accounting courses and statistics classes in an effort to overcome the weakness. In the meantime, the time and energy put into compensating for the weak area might have been much better spent in honing the strong areas.

At other times the pressure to cover up the weakness comes not from within, but from outside sources. For example, a shortsighted manager who wants all his employees to conform to one particular model might demand that every person be equally skilled in a variety of areas. But no matter what model he chooses, there will be a lot more people who don't conform to it than who do. Consequently, no one on his staff gets to focus on strengths and, instead, must continually run a mental obstacle course to deal with a variety of things that are perceived as neither essential nor enjoyable.

The best thing a business or individual can do is to focus on developing strengths. Let the numbers people cut loose on numbers. Let the team players rub shoulders as often as possible. Leave the creative people alone long enough to come up with some wonderful, original, profitable ideas. Trying to perpetually compensate for weaknesses brings productivity to a crawl. But allowing everyone to focus on individual strengths as much as possible forms an unbelievable synergy. Not only does productivity skyrocket, but morale and motivation go up as well.

Of course, the key to success is putting the right people together to form teams that cover all the necessary bases. (See chapter 13.)

Differences relate to personal, social, and occupational behavior.

In the last chapter you saw how, in certain circumstances, people sometimes choose to behave in a way that doesn't particularly reflect their true feelings or needs. We called this *socialized behavior.*

It is important to be clear at this point. I am not suggesting that individuals are "cut from the same cloth" and then choose to be different. Rather, I believe that behind the socialized behavior of each individual is the underlying, unique, genuine personality. This is the behavior that will, in most cases, hold true whether the person is functioning independently, in a social group, or at work. He or she may adopt a mode of socialized behavior in any of these settings, of course. And though observers may make incorrect assumptions based on the behavior, the person almost always knows when he is going against his natural uniqueness.

Some of our consultants refer to socialized behavior as "courtship behavior." Perhaps we never work harder to hide who we really are than during the period we begin dating and into the first few months of marriage. We want so much to impress the other person that we are afraid to show any sign of vulnerability or weakness. Of course, such an intense cover-up cannot go on forever. So sometime shortly after the honeymoon, many people are in for a big shock. Both individuals, who have been working so hard to be perpetually appealing, can keep up the charade no longer. They revert to their actual selves with the harsh reality of Cinderella at midnight. It is quite common for people at this stage to wonder, *Who is this person I married?* ("Courtship behavior" is also typical of applicants during job interviews and throughout the first month or so of employment.)

So whether you are thinking through personal issues or relating to friends and coworkers, I urge you to cherish the characteristics that make you unique. There will certainly be times when socialized behavior is advisable, or even necessary. But there will also be many times when you can choose to let down the walls and allow the people around you to see who you really are. The sooner you become comfortable in sharing your differences with the others around you, the happier you are going to be.

Individuals can manage their behavior.

Another important result of knowing yourself well enough to distinguish between your strengths and weaknesses is that you can adapt to situations where you must operate in a way you don't particularly enjoy. Let's say you report to someone whose main goal in life is to impress her boss (the vice president). She therefore has you and all your peers conform to what she thinks would impress the VP. As a result, you all have to fill out time-consuming (but useless) reports, attend numerous scheduling and planning meetings, and perform other various "jump-through-the-hoop" tasks.

If you haven't identified the things that make you special and unique (regardless of whether or not your boss notices), you may feel a great deal of pressure to perform and behave exactly as instructed. Your self-image is placed in the hands of your inconsistent and insensitive boss, so you never feel good about yourself.

But if you know what you do well, you can step out of your most productive mode from time to time, knowing that you must do so to accommodate your pesky boss. The things you do purely for show and out of obligation will get done, but you know that's not the stuff you're building a reputation on. If your boss's boss is impressed, fine. If not, that's fine too. You have a more well-defined sense of what is truly important.

When a person is able to voluntarily act in a way that goes against his or her personal, preferred style, we call it "managing behavior." Not only are people capable of doing this, but it is important that they learn to do so. From time to time we are all called on to perform in a way that is unnatural to us. By keeping in mind that this does not reflect who we really are, we can cope much better with our assignments. We know that when we finish, we can revert to our natural, unique behavior.

People need opportunities for personal growth.

It's a real shame when business leaders don't know (or don't care) about the unique skills and interests of their employees. Some would be quite shocked if they could get a glimpse of their workers' home lives. The man who works quietly in a windowless office may take his family on frequent outdoor jaunts—camping, sailing, mountain climbing, rafting. The woman who has been repeatedly passed over for promotion due to apparent lack of interest may be running a separate business out of her home. The young executive whom the bosses hope to motivate with lures of big raises and high position may spend most nights and weekends doing church or social work.

Employees can be coerced to adapt to corporate expectations through intimidation, financial need, or any number of other reasons. But they will also find ways to exercise their unique skills and behaviors. If work does not provide a valid outlet, they will look elsewhere. The problem, then, does not lie with the individual, but with the organization. When a person has identified what he or she is best at and *enjoys* doing, a wise company is going to try very hard to find a position to maximize the person's potential. The better a company gets at matching people to jobs, the better it will be for both employer and employee.

You can be sure that the person *will* find an outlet for his strengths and interests. If it's not with your company, it may well be with a competitor.

Every organization has its distinctive personality.

Just as individuals have specific strengths and personalities, so do businesses and even informal groups. The next chapter will go into greater detail to categorize broad and general personality types. But at this point it is enough to be aware that repeatable and definable traits will emerge from any group of people who spend time together. If a specific style of behavior isn't mandated from the top and if people don't have to continually perform to such expectations, then the personality of the company will become a combination of individuals' strengths and behaviors.

In some cases the personality of the company will be quite apparent. IBM has worked hard to establish its image and personality. When you think of them, you think pin-stripe suits and professional demeanor. Accounting firms are another group who try to project a no-nonsense personality. Marketing companies generally have more of an upbeat, go-get-'em personality.

In other cases, the organizational personality is a matter of choice. A restaurant, for example, can present an informal family-style personality, a wacky good-place-to-take-a-date ambiance, a formal fine-dining-experience personality, or any variation in between. Sometimes an organization finds it beneficial to go "against type" in order to stand out from others in its field. A bank, for instance, might challenge employees to go out of their way to evoke a fun and friendly atmosphere rather than a formal ("stuffy") one. This trend is true of some malls now that include ice rinks or even huge theme parks to narrow the lines between shopping and entertainment.

But even if your company consists of only two people who lick envelopes for a living, it will have its own special personality. Whenever leaders read that companies who want to be effective and productive should do one thing or another, they need to be careful in following such advice. Many a company whose strength lay in its unique personality has been all but ruined by a misguided manager who tried to follow someone's "secrets" to squeeze out an extra percent of profit.

Be aware that there are many myths that can damage a company's (or an individual's) strongest point—its innate, unique personality. One of the best ways to debunk myths is to identify and respect the behaviors and personalities that don't match your own. It is to that purpose we turn in the next chapter.

CHAPTER 4

WHAT'S YOUR COLOR?

So far, the discussion of personality and perception has been quite general. But in the next few chapters, we will zero in on specific categories of personality. Keep in mind that I am in no way suggesting that there is a limit on the number of possible "normal" or "right" behaviors. Rather, I hope to show how the unlimited number of normal and right behaviors people display can be categorized to some extent. Do you recognize yourself or others in the following descriptions?

Greta is a born salesperson. She would rather talk with other people than eat. Every time you see her she is selling, persuading, promoting, motivating, counseling, teaching, or working with people in some way to get results. When she believes in a product, service, or idea, she can sell it. If you want to win friends and influence people, Greta is the person for the job.

Ray is a doer. He works, talks, and lives fast. He makes quick decisions and organizes others to get results. You can read Ray's thoughts by the way he acts. He's very direct. He enjoys building, organizing, working with his hands, solving practical problems, and having an end product he can see and feel. He's objective, competitive, and commanding. If you want something done quickly, Ray's your man.

Yvonne is a good person to have in your corner on April 15! She loves working with rules, definitions, processes, and details. So she's happy handling tax returns, scheduling, detailed calculations, record-keeping, and systematic procedures. She's also a good person to consult on financial matters, because she is always cautious and thorough in her analysis.

Blake is the best idea person around. He is creative, innovative, and an excellent long-range planner. He enjoys abstract ideas and finding new ways to solve problems. Instead of spinning his wheels in useless activity, he'd rather lean back, think the problem through, and come up with the most viable option for solving it.

After reading these descriptions, perhaps you're still tempted to think that one of these four people has the "best" profile, while the other personalities are less desirable. If so, maybe you need to reread the previous chapter before moving on. We *must* learn to ignore the myths that are so prevalent in our society and our business cultures. Unless we place a high value on each of these personality types, we will do the others a grave injustice. And even though we may not intentionally devalue a person, the wrong assumptions we make, based on our perceptions of that personality, are likely to influence our attitudes and behaviors toward that person.

Don't allow your judgment to be colored—that is, unless you are willing to color it in one of four ways. Let me explain.

If you were to drop by our office one day and eavesdrop for a while, you might get the idea that our employees were speaking in code. (Actually, that wouldn't be a bad perception.) You'd be likely to hear things such as:

- "You're behaving very red for a blue today."

- "All this yellow work is the least favorite part of my job, but it has to be done."

- "She is being very green today. I can't get a word in edgewise."

At the very core of the Birkman personality evaluation process is a four-color grid (like the one on the back cover of this book). Rather than assigning names for various personality types, we have simply designated the types by color. This may sound simple—even simplistic—at first, but using colors can be a practical time-saver. For example: You are approaching a busy intersection at rush hour. Hundreds of other drivers are attempting to move their vehicles from one place to another, as quickly as possible, and they're all funneling through this single spot. But above the intersection hangs a traffic light. When the light turns green, the drivers proceed past the intersection. When it turns red, they stop. Since everyone understands and conforms to this system, the traffic continues to move smoothly and efficiently. What could be simpler?

In developing our system of personality assessment, we have not applied the principles of industrial psychology—the effects of various colors on mood, productivity, and so forth. Yet while colors can be more significant than we may realize, this is not the important issue. We have simply selected basic colors to represent four general groupings of personalities.

At this point skeptics may be thinking, *Here we go again. Four categories of behavior. I've been through all this before.* If so, I ask you to bear with me. True, it's not uncommon for authors to classify behaviors or personalities into four basic groups. But while this is the ultimate result of many studies, it is just the starting point for us. Our four-color Life Style Grid is only a foundation upon which we will build additional layers of more complex and eye-opening revelations about an individual's personality.

Below is our basic grid. It is divided into four quadrants, with a different color for each section. The next chapter will begin to plot additional points on the grid, but for now we will deal with the basics. The more nearly you resemble the personality defined by the traits at the top of the grid, the more inclined you are to use direct communication (as opposed to indirect communication at the bottom). The left side of the grid indicates a strong task orientation, while the qualities on the right translate into a more intense desire to work with people.

The four people previously described—Greta, Ray, Yvonne, and Blake—correspond to the colors on the grid that begin with the first

letter of their names (Green, Red, Yellow, and Blue). Greta (Green) is in the upper right quadrant, indicating both a desire to communicate directly and to work with people. Ray (Red) also prefers direct communication, but his attention is devoted more to the task at hand. To him, people are likely to be viewed much as any other "tool"—simply a means to help him accomplish his objective. Yvonne (Yellow) is most comfortable with indirect communication (forms, rules and regulations, etc.) and when dealing with a task. Blake (Blue) is innovative and introspective, yet may well need to be around people to trigger the creative spark he needs.

As you can see, the *feelings* of people in adjoining upper and lower quadrants are about the same. And the *actions* of people in adjoining side-by-side quadrants are the same. Therefore, the types of personalities that are most different are the ones in diagonal quadrants. Another way to think of this is to be aware that wherever the colors touch, there will be a certain amount of crossover between either actions or feelings. Where only the corners touch, there is usually only a very small degree of similarity between personality types.

When you know where you fit on the grid, you can better understand why you do some of the things you do. In addition, you can begin to understand why other people do some of the things *they* do. Recognizing that someone is a "Yellow" or a "Blue," a "Red" or a "Green" will provide significant insight as to what that person expects or prefers, and how you can best relate to him or her.

Again, let me repeat that these are merely generalizations. I am *not* saying that there are four—and only four—kinds of people. I believe that every individual is wonderfully unique and complex. However, as we begin to paint a personality "group portrait" with very broad strokes, we can start with these four basic colors (groups).

I am not attempting to suggest that all creative people (Blue) detest hands-on experiences (Red behavior). Someone who is comfortable with people (Green) can also be a whiz with numbers (Yellow) or extremely creative (Blue). But most people are going to gravitate to one of these quadrants and feel most comfortable there.

Chapters 5 and 6 will begin to differentiate between an individual's interests, outward behavior, and needs. These considerations may be localized within the same color on the grid, or they may span two or three other colors.

Finding Your Color

Receiving a personalized, individual assessment is the best way to learn which of the four quadrants is most indicative of your own personality. Yet in lieu of such an assessment, there are two other ways to help determine your self-perception. One way is to answer the sixteen True/False questions below, which are taken from the more extensive Birkman Questionnaire. Another is to read the explanations and examples given in this book. These descriptions provide more in-depth understanding about the dimensions of each type of person.

Most people will discover that their answers to the sixteen questions will validate and reinforce the beliefs they now hold about themselves as they have read thus far in the chapter. Others, however, may find that the results of their mini-questionnaires differ from how they see themselves based on other descriptions in the book. Since every individual is a complex being, the descriptions in these chapters are probably a more reliable indication of one's true perceptions and motivations than this simple test.

The Birkman Method and its wide range of reports and applications listed in the appendices provide more extensive and reliable indications. The sample questions below are to "whet your appetite" to learn more, not to replace the more extensive and dependable assessment reports. Take a few minutes to answer the questions.

How Do You See Yourself?

Copyright 1994, Birkman & Associates, Inc. Houston, Texas.

Here are some statements about *yourself.* Read each statement carefully. Please mark every statement, even when you are in doubt.

If you feel a statement is *True* or *Mostly True,* circle the T. If you feel a statement is *False* or *Mostly False,* circle the F.

GROUP 1
1. Argue when contradicted.   T   F
2. Openly express differences of opinion with groups
   and individuals.   T   F
3. Argue a point when I know I am right.   T   F
4. Tell a person what I think of him when annoyed.   T   F

5.	Bluff to get what I want.	T	F
6.	Put annoying people in their places.	T	F
7.	Help friends by pointing out their faults.	T	F
8.	Keep others guessing.	T	F

GROUP 2

9.	Like firm and strict supervision.	T	F
10.	Orderly and systematic.	T	F
11.	Seldom leave things until the last minute.	T	F
12.	Want to be early for appointments.	T	F
13.	Work for accuracy rather than speed.	T	F
14.	Like to finish a job I've started even though others lose patience with me.	T	F
15.	Can schedule my time for a week or longer and stick with it.	T	F
16.	Prefer to take care of the details rather than take things as they come.	T	F

When you have completed all sixteen questions, total the number of *True* answers in each section. Then check your score against the following scale to determine in which quadrant of the grid you may belong.

True Answers Only

Group 1	Group 2	COLOR	JOB CATEGORY
5 or more	and 5 or more	Red	Production-Centered
4 or less	and 5 or more	Yellow	Procedure-Centered
5 or more	and 4 or less	Green	People-Centered
4 or less	and 4 or less	Blue	Idea-Centered

Some scores fall very clearly in one category or another. For instance, a score of 1–6 (one *True* response in Group 1 and six *True* responses in Group 2) indicates someone who is strongly "Yellow." Similarly, a score of 5–2 is clearly a "Green" score. Other scores are less definitive. People whose Group 1 scores are 3 or 4, or whose Group 2 scores are 4 or 5, should be aware that they have traits of more than one category. A change in only one or two answers would place them in a different color code; therefore, these individuals should pay close attention to the descriptions of the other colors as well.

To see if you agree with the results of your mini-questionnaire, check the following grid, which shows the usual styles of each color quadrant. Remember: If your numeric score was close to a number that might have placed you in another quadrant, you may have characteristics from that quadrant as well.

Assertive

Usual styles	Usual styles
Friendly	Competitive
Decisive and energetic	Assertive
Frank	Flexible
Logical	Enthusiastic about new things
Usual styles	Usual styles
Orderly	Insightful
Concentrative	Selectively sociable
Cautious	Thoughtful
Insistent	Reflective
	Optimistic

Low-key

Do you agree with the characteristics that are associated with your color quadrant? The mini-questionnaire has done well at seminars we hold, but your results would be much more accurate after completing the full questionnaire.

Relating to Others

In a company, church, or family, knowing each other's colors can be very helpful. Not only can you begin to understand yourself a bit more, but you will also have a better idea of how to relate to others.

How to Relate to Yellows

Remember, "Yellows" prefer, and even enjoy, having a set procedure for everything. They like numbers, rules, and structure. So when you relate to Yellows, here are a few suggestions:

1. Build relationships around task-oriented projects.
2. Outline the task and let them find practical methods for accomplishing it.
3. Challenge them to outline specific objectives and solutions to problems.
4. Allow space and interact rationally and objectively.
5. Alleviate worry by having a clear-cut strategy.
6. Outline a tangible goal.
7. Draw on their ability to analyze.
8. Take the initiative, but let them suggest alternatives.

How to Relate to Greens

These are the conversational, quick-decision-makers. If you're not a Green as well, it may be difficult for you to try to keep up with these individuals. But here are some recommendations to help you get started:

1. Interact by expressing your concerns and sharing feelings.
2. Realize the importance of recognition, compliments, and appreciation.
3. Show an interest and allow them to talk.
4. Expect them to get involved and interact.

5. Capitalize on Greens' ease in relating to others and making them comfortable.
6. Count on their eager assistance.
7. Use their talent for enlivening and entertaining in social situations.
8. Tell them how they can help, and draw on their practical applications.

How to Relate to Reds

Reds generally enjoy building, organizing, and seeing projects through to completion. They are direct in their approach to problems and people, so don't be put off by them. Here are some suggestions:

1. Act, react, and respond to their initiative.
2. Challenge and confront them.
3. Be forceful, direct, and straightforward.
4. Identify the need or the problem for them, and then hang on as they go to work.
5. Draw on their expertise in promoting change and new concepts.
6. Recognize their practical leadership potential and give support.
7. Stay involved to give additional/balancing viewpoints when new challenges arise.
8. Avoid lengthy explanations and sentiment.

How to Relate to Blues

When dealing with "Blue" people, you might need to check occasionally to make sure you've still got their attention. Their minds have a tendency to springboard from whatever you're saying to dozens of other things at a moment's notice. To keep them on track, try these ideas:

1. Relate to them in a quiet way.
2. Run your plan by them for consideration.
3. Involve them in the planning.
4. Outline the project and allow them to take the initiative.
5. Ask them to help in ways directly related to their talents.

6. Give justified support and encouragement.
7. Show deserved appreciation by being a friend.
8. Make use of their ideas and creativity.

Color Contrasts

Suppose there are nine cats in a house and it is your task to get them out. How would you go about it?

If you are an autocratic doer (Red), you are action-oriented and strong-willed. Your approach might be to go into the house, bellow "Scat!" and expect the cats to get out if they know what's good for them! You would show those cats that you mean business, and you wouldn't waste time getting the job done.

If you are more of a detail person (Yellow), you would first plan your work and then work your plan. You would probably require a system of cat removal. So you might begin by assigning numbers to the cats—one through nine—and labeling each one with a name tag (in calligraphy): Cat #1, Cat #2, Cat #3, etc. Next you would provide nine neat holes in the wall, also well-labeled in bold numbers. Then you would teach each cat the appropriate route of exit. (It's not enough for the cats to get out; the removal must be done *properly.*) So you will be completely frustrated if, for instance, Cat #3 goes out Exit #7.

If your approach to situations is that of an enthusiastic salesperson (Green), you would feel a sense of empathy for those poor cats who are confined in that nasty old house when they could be outside instead. You would want to "sell" them on the sunshine, fresh air, and other benefits. In your emotionally charged approach, you would be likely to prop open all the doors and windows, place warm milk and cat food outside each opening, and stand by to coax them, "Here, kitty, kitty!"

And if your personality leans toward that of the artistic, poetic, philosopher type (Blue), you are intensely aware of beauty, reverence, creativity, and awe. You enjoy quiet and pensive moments of solitude, when you can tune into the wonders of the universe and the mysteries of life. So when confronted with the cats-in-the-house dilemma, your response is likely to be, "What in the world am I doing worrying about cats?"

Below are some additional examples of how to differentiate between the various "colors" of personality. As you read through them, see if they help you confirm the color quadrant you've slotted for yourself.

Primary Interest When Reading Books

Red: Action
Green: Characters
Blue: Ideas
Yellow: Story line

Response When Anxieties Rise and Defense Mechanisms Take Over

Red: Pushes harder and takes *some* kind of action.
Green: Feelings get hurt and needs to talk out the problem.
Blue: Withdraws and mulls it over . . . and over.
Yellow: Hides behind the system and begins to reorganize.

Slogans to Live By

Red: When in doubt, run in circles and scream and shout!
Green: Listen, Lord, your servant speaketh.
Blue: Think twice, act once.
Yellow: If it ain't broke, don't try to fix it.

Variations of the Golden Rule

Red: Do unto others before they do unto you.
Green: Do unto others, do unto others, do unto others.
Blue: Do unto others as they do unto you.
Yellow: Do unto others and report back to me.

Mental Questions on the Way to a Party

Red: Will there be some movers and shakers there?
Green: Is this going to be a fun, interesting group?

Blue: Will there be someone there I can feel close to?
Yellow: Who planned this affair? Will it go according to schedule?

How a Sense of Significance Is Attained

Red: Status
Green: Popularity
Blue: The love and respect of a few key individuals
Yellow: Security

Negotiating Techniques

Red: Bartering
Green: Persuasion
Blue: New ideas
Yellow: Facts

We will be making several important distinctions in the next chapters that will help you clarify some of the observations you have been making about yourself and others. Yet you should be able to tell by now that most individuals have definable, repeatable, and even somewhat predictable behaviors. We all make perceptions based on each other's behaviors, and connected to our perceptions are a number of assumptions about ourselves and other people.

As I mentioned earlier, associating with a color on our grid is simply a beginning as you make some initial assumptions (educated guesses) about your personality profile. The next two chapters will help you build on what you've already learned and will help you make additional distinctions. So don't be too concerned if, at this point, you still have more questions than answers.

It could get depressing to go through life thinking, *I'm creative, so I obviously can't be a good people person.* Or, *Gee, I really enjoy doing things according to a system, so I guess I shouldn't pursue that job in sales that sounds so appealing to me.* I hope to show you that by zeroing in on specific strengths, your choices will become much more varied and specific—not at all limiting.

CHAPTER 5

INTERESTS

Human behavior is an amazing and fascinating field of study, and one doesn't have to be a professional psychologist to appreciate it. The next time you're in an airport or mall, try this experiment. Try to discover as much as possible about the people around you simply by watching their behavior.

What do they reveal to you about the things they are interested in? T-shirts with brand endorsements or slogans? Tie pins that reflect golf, tennis, or some other pastime? Shopping bags from specialty stores? Books or magazines that relate to specific activities? Do you observe any nervous habits—tapping feet, drumming fingers, pacing— that would indicate the person is under stress? Which ones would you say are currently under the most stress? What might you guess your "subjects" do for a living? (Salespeople tend to be on the phone a lot. Accountants may pull out their calculators. Artists, designers, writers, or architects may be using pencil and paper to capture ideas for later development.)

If you try this experiment, you may be surprised at some of your discoveries. First, you may find that people reveal more about themselves than you might have expected. Secondly, you should begin to discover some things about *yourself*. By intentionally trying to analyze other people through nonverbal and instinctive methods, you may recognize some of your own repeated behaviors.

Much of what we do is so habitual that we don't even realize we're doing it. Sometimes this can be advantageous. For example, most of us have developed the most efficient routine for getting ready to go to work. We no longer need to give much thought to shaving, showering, or dressing. And because we know almost to the minute how much time each activity will require, we can spend any additional time as we wish. We can hit the snooze alarm a couple of times before having to get up, or we can spend those extra moments with spouse and children. Similar routines save time at work or in completing chores where repetition is necessary. At other times, however, our force-of-habit behaviors are not beneficial. Perhaps we wish we could eliminate certain compulsive behavior, yet can't seem to help ourselves no matter what we try.

And how do you behave when you're under stress? Have you noticed that other people seem to respond the same way to stressful situations—perhaps in ways that are nonproductive? Do you detect any similar programmed responses to stress in your own life, even though you know they aren't desirable—responses you'd certainly like to correct?

If so, you're not alone. The very thing that makes human nature so interesting—the uniqueness of our personalities—is the thing that occasionally makes our lives so complicated. It is difficult to begin to break down our behaviors into areas that help us understand ourselves and our actions. Yet it *can* be done.

I believe we can begin to see our personalities more clearly, and clarify our perceptions about ourselves and each other, by examining four areas:

(1) Interests,
(2) Effective operating style,
(3) Needs, and
(4) Stress (reactive behavior).

The variables within each of these areas are what make you a unique and special individual. The better you can define yourself in each of these categories, the better you will be able to understand why you do the things you do (and what makes others seem so unusual).

Again, until you have the opportunity to fill out a complete Birkman Method questionnaire, you won't be able to determine *exactly* where you would rate in each of the four areas. But you can gain much insight by studying the breakdown of each of the classifications in the mini-questionnaire (pages 42–43). Once you know what to look for, you remove much of the complexity of understanding yourself.

This chapter will deal with the category of Interests. The next chapter will cover the other three areas. While discussing interests, I will try to use definitions that are broad enough to cover job as well as personal preferences. So let's start by saying that interests are simply *those activities which provide the greatest sense of personal fulfillment—the things you most enjoy doing.*

If we go back to the grid quadrants, thinking in terms of interests, here's what a broad breakdown would look like:

Summary

Red

If your color is Red, your interests are in the area of **getting things done**. Regardless of the actual job you do, you are likely to describe your goals in terms of a finished product, practical solutions, or working with things.

Green

If your color is Green, your interests are in the area of **directly interacting with or influencing people.** Again, your job may not involve you in this work, but you will probably describe your objectives in terms of the people you work with or for.

Yellow

If your color is Yellow, you are concerned about **structure, precedent, or routine.** Your objectives are likely associated with establishing a code, set of rules of procedures, or formalizing your work or the work of others.

Blue

If your color is Blue, you are interested in **creative or innovative activities.** Your personal work objectives have to do with planning for the future, expressing ideas artistically, and creativity.

Ten Classifications of Interests

As you can see, the four quadrants represent broad areas of interest. Yet to help determine which quadrant a person is most likely to fit, our questionnaire singles out ten separate and distinct variables. These varied interests are listed below.

Read the descriptions carefully, taking note of the level of your identification with each of the broad categories. Then rank the ten interests in ascending order from one ("I have low identification with this interest") to ten ("I have high identification with this interest").

Artistic

Characteristics: An affinity for abstract concepts and unique forms usually demonstrated in a visible manner. Involves being creative, thinking up new procedures, planning, expressing ideas artistically, enjoying beauty, and working with visual things.

Possible Occupations: Photographer, architect, artist, florist, designer, painter, decorator.

Possible Hobbies: Painting, sculpture, crafts, photography, ceramics, weaving, raising prize-winning flowers, restoring antiques, collecting art, designing clothing.

Clerical

Characteristics: Has an affinity for order, structure, and accessibility of material and information. Expressed through working with records and procedures, scheduling activities and resources, filing, systematizing materials, keeping close control over resources, producing order in the surrounding environment, etc.

Possible Occupations: Secretary, typist, office worker, financial manager.

Possible Hobbies: Setting up a great home filing system, understanding tax and insurance forms, compiling scrapbooks.

Literary

Characteristics: Has an affinity for language and its use in the printed word, along with appreciation for the abstract feelings and ideas conveyed in written material. Expressed through reading in all forms (pamphlets, novels, professional publications, biographies, etc.), concern with different literary styles, interest in writers and their histories, writing or a desire to write, foreign language, etc.

Possible Occupations: Writer, editor, literary scholar, reporter, librarian.

Possible Hobbies: Reading (whether Zane Grey or Émile Zola), writing letters, keeping a diary or journal, writing amateur plays, working crossword puzzles, playing word games such as Scrabble.

Mechanical

Characteristics: Has an affinity for the design, building, and/or maintenance of equipment requiring the operation of several interrelated parts with separate functions. Expressed through activities that involve hands-on participation or analysis of how things work.

Possible Occupations: Engineer, machine designer, auto mechanic, carpenter, pilot, plumber, craftsperson.

Possible Hobbies: Home repair, car maintenance, observing construction activities or mechanical operations, woodworking, building model airplanes.

Musical

Characteristics: Has an affinity for the art of arranging sound in time through the elements of rhythm, melody, harmony, and color. Expressed through enjoyment of these activities—not necessarily having a talent for them.
Possible Occupations: Professional singer, musician, songwriter.
Possible Hobbies: Playing a musical instrument, listening to various forms of music, songwriting, singing, dancing, attending concerts and musicals.

Numerical

Characteristics: Has an affinity for activities requiring quantitative or mathematical abilities (i.e., the use of numbers). Expressed through bookkeeping, statistical theory, systems approaches, any measurement technique, logic and forms of logic expression, sequencing events, novel approaches to measurement, etc.
Possible Occupations: Cashier, accountant, mathematician, administrative office worker.
Possible Hobbies: Cryptography (making and breaking codes), sports statistics, counted cross-stitch needlework, working with computers.

Outdoor

Characteristics: Has an affinity for any activities that are conducted in the outdoors. Expressed through physical activity in a natural environment.
Possible Occupations: Carpenter, farmer, animal trainer, sportsman, forest ranger, tree surgeon, oil field worker, fisherman, field engineer.
Possible Hobbies: Sailing, skiing, camping, hiking, fishing, swimming, hunting, gardening, driving or touring, certain kinds of sports, building

a retreat or lake house, observing or reading naturalist materials, specimen-collecting (mushrooms, insects, etc.), painting landscapes.

Persuasive

Characteristics: Has an affinity for any activities that relate to communicating, working, relating, interacting with others in a manner requiring the use of influence. Involves convincing others to accept a product, service, or idea as well as discussing, observing the interaction of others, and studying people.

Possible Occupations: Salesperson, teacher, psychological counselor, public relations director, politician, store manager, radio announcer, auctioneer.

Possible Hobbies: Debating, visiting with friends, putting together a Neighborhood Watch program, campaigning for a political candidate, fundraising, negotiating.

Scientific

Characteristics: Has an affinity for any area of study dealing with a body of facts systematically arranged to show the operation of laws. Expressed through chemistry, physics, medicine, biology, anthropology, astronomy, botany, zoology, geographics, reading or viewing science-related events or materials, etc.

Possible Occupations: Diagnostician, scientist, lab worker, detective, meteorologist, dentist, any number of medical and technical jobs.

Possible Hobbies: Star-gazing, doing chemistry experiments, cooking, developing your own photographs.

Social Services

Characteristics: Has an affinity for those activities that tend to indirectly assist others in obtaining goals of growth, development, or physical necessities. Expressed through social work, church groups and activities, civic groups, youth services, volunteer work, etc.

Possible Occupations: Teacher, social worker, public service worker, counselor, personnel or employment manager.

Possible Hobbies: Leading a Scout troop, doing charitable and volunteer work, listening and advising when friends have problems.

Now, using the checklist below, rank these broad categories of interests in ascending order, from 1 (low) to 10 (high). In other words, if you have the least amount of interest in Outdoor, for example, rate it number 1. If your greatest interest is Musical, rate it number 10. Be as accurate as possible. The resultant self-understanding will be well worth the effort.

_____ Artistic
_____ Clerical
_____ Literary
_____ Mechanical
_____ Musical
_____ Numerical
_____ Outdoor
_____ Persuasive
_____ Scientific
_____ Social Services

Now that you have completed your ranking, you will be interested to learn—based on our extensive testing and research—which interests are predominant by color:

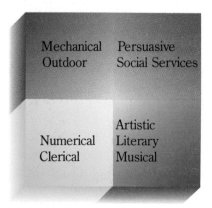

Scientific interest can show up in any of the color quadrants. Your interests are *you*. In many ways they determine how well you live, how satisfied and fulfilled you are, and how you measure your self-worth. When you know your interests, you know who you are.

No doubt, as you looked through this list, you did a fairly good job of ranking the interests from one to ten in order of your own personal preferences. Yet most people who are tested are surprised to find that at least one area is ranked either higher or lower than they would have expected.

A strong interest has the status of a **need,** and the person should actively seek an outlet for this interest—at work, at home, or during leisure hours. Particularly in stress situations (e.g., unemployment) is it important to fulfill these interests.

My company's consultants cite dozens of stories to illustrate the importance of pursuing one's interests. Here's just one:

> The head nurse at a local hospital, deciding that she could no longer take the stress of her administrative responsibilities, told her boss that she wanted to step down and go back into nursing. The boss, unwilling to lose a valuable employee, came to us for advice. At our request, the nurse filled out the Birkman assessment questionnaire, which confirmed that she had high management scores and would appear to be in a job that was a good fit for her personality. However, in the Interests section, we also noted high scores in Outdoor (99 percent) and Artistic (98 percent).
>
> In a subsequent interview, we questioned her about these areas. When asked if she ever got outdoors, she replied, somewhat sarcastically, "I'm divorced and I have two kids. When am I going to get outside?" I asked if she ever dabbled in art, and her reply was the same, "When am I ever going to find time to paint?"
>
> At this point I asked her to postpone her job transfer for three months and try an experiment. She agreed to do so. In the meantime, she was to enroll herself and her children in weekend classes at the Y. She could get back into oil painting while her kids pursued their own interests.
>
> Next we consulted with the nurse's boss. When asked what he

could do to get his employee outside more often, he remembered a corporate gazebo that was seldom used. Since the hospital was located in the Houston area, he determined to hold all meetings outdoors, weather permitting. Then, as if a light bulb went on in his head, he told me of a small upstairs storage room with three windows. Not long afterward, he had the room converted into a new office for the nurse.

When we met with her three months later, she was a different person. "I love my job," she said, "and I don't know what got into me. I guess I just didn't realize how much I had denied my interests."

Our interests influence us much more than we realize, and though it may seem impossible to make time for everything in our busy schedules, it's important to pursue hobbies or other areas of interest. While most of us have to work for a living, make house or apartment payments, prepare for retirement, and/or raise a family, much of the wonderful uniqueness of each person lies in his or her **interests.** To neglect this area is to invite frustration, burnout, irritability, or worse.

And it's not as if the problem is limited to the lower rungs of the employment ladder. Top-level executives, too, have had to learn this lesson the hard way. At one Texas bank, a vice president who was about to be terminated for unsatisfactory job performance, was advised to devote some of his time to his hobby. His attitude and behavior changed dramatically after he got back into his art work, and his job was saved.

In another case, the problem was with the president of the company. He couldn't be fired since he owned the company. Yet those who reported to him claimed that he was one of the most difficult people they had ever tried to work for. When his staff discovered that his Birkman scores in Artistic interests were extremely high, they bought and presented him with a set of paints and brushes, easel, smock—the works. Soon after he took up his art again, his management style mellowed and his employees were much happier.

When you identify your strongest interests, the best possible option is to find a job that allows you to develop them in a profitable way. Many times this can be done by restructuring your current job, changing jobs within your company, or even sending out resumés to find something more suited to your interests. Sometimes, however, it is impossible to find a job that allows you to pursue your personal interests in a work environment. In such cases, it is imperative for you to develop those interests on your own. Get up earlier, stay up later, carve out some time on the weekends, or do whatever it takes. You'll soon discover that the investment of time and effort will pay off in renewed energy and purpose.

You are at the mercy of other people in many areas of your life. But staying in touch with your interests is not something anyone else will ever force you to do. If *you* don't take the initiative in doing the things that are most important to you, years can pass without your knowing the satisfaction of being who you really are.

CHAPTER 6

STYLES, NEEDS, AND STRESS

A man once found a book in the attic of an old house. The pages were yellow with age and tended to crumble as he turned them. Try as he might, he was able to make out only one paragraph of what was written: On the shores of the Black Sea was a pebble that, in the hands of the person who possessed it, could turn anything it touched into gold. According to the ancient writer, this pebble could be distinguished from others only by holding it, for unlike the other pebbles, it would be warm to the touch.

After reading of this amazing secret, the man immediately went to the Black Sea and began to search for the pebble. From morning to night he worked, picking up pebbles one by one and feeling for the sensation of warmth. To ensure that he didn't pick up the same pebble twice, he would fling each examined pebble far out into the sea.

Days stretched into weeks, weeks into months, and months into years. The man continued looking for that one special pebble. But every one he picked up was as cold as ice, and he flung it away as fast as he picked it up. By now he had become so expert that he could pick up a pebble and fling it into the sea with one smooth action.

One evening, at the end of another long day, the man was preparing to leave the beach. One last pebble lay in front of him. He picked it up and with his perfected motion threw it far out into the sea. But as he watched it splash down into the deep and murky water, he realized that *it was the warm pebble he had been searching for!*

Like the man in the story, we believe that discovering the right "pebble" can change our lives. Yet we may fail to recognize it when we find it and may throw it away in the process! Not many of us have a clue as to how to break free of the habits we've established over a lifetime. I believe such freedom is possible, however, even though it may not be easy. And like every other problem, the first step is to gather as much information as possible. We can't change what we're doing until we're able to truly know ourselves and identify our behaviors.

To do so, we will use the same approach in this chapter as we used in the previous chapter on identifying interests. We will break down a complex topic into smaller, more understandable components. And we will "get our feet wet" gradually by starting with a familiar topic before moving on to more challenging areas.

Effective Operating Style

One's effective operating style, *active behavior*, is one's best behavior. It's how you act when you feel good about yourself and are enjoying the demands of the situation you are dealing with. It's how you respond when you perceive that most of your personal and psychological needs are being met. Active behavior is:

- positive in nature

- accepted as positive by others

- flexible

- easy and natural

- easily modified by experience

Based on what you have learned about the personality types represented by the four colors of the Birkman grid, you may already have a feel for what the effective operating style would be for each category. Check your instincts against the following profiles.

Red Operating Style

People in this quadrant thrive on power, authority, and dominance. A Red will usually deal with other people in a direct, assertive manner and not tolerate poor performance from anyone, self included. A Red person likes:
 group attention
 decisive action
 physical activity
 challenging tasks
 competitive situations
 matter-of-fact relationships

Green Operating Style

If Greens learn to manage their style effectively, they can charm people into accomplishing almost anything. Green people tend to influence the behavior and attitudes of others. A Green person likes:
 a worthy cause
 novelty and change
 authoritative support
 discussion and debate
 personal understanding
 a sense of personal freedom

Yellow Operating Style

A Yellow person keeps a very low profile, yet understands systems and procedures in a way a Green person does not. Yellow people are very comfortable with the status quo. They like:
 group backing
 minimum change
 group approval

consistent controls
systems and procedures

Blue Operating Style

A Blue person is future-oriented and likes to explore the implications of tomorrow. Blue people are creative, artistic, and innovative. A Blue person likes:
    service activities
    unhurried decisions
    pleasant relationships
    approval from individuals
    suggestions rather than orders

The previous descriptions refer to what people *like,* usually internal assessments. Yet when people are feeling good about themselves and able to be in their effective operating styles, they usually display discernible *outward* behaviors as well. Some of these are shown in the following chart:

Objective about people	Personable
Commanding	Directive
Competitive	Outspoken
Practical	Independent
Forceful	Enthusiastic
Sociable	Perceptive
Orderly	Agreeable
Cooperative	Conscientious
Consistent	Reflective, creative
Cautious	Cautious

While these observations of outward behavior are usually accurate, the observer cannot tell much about the person's inner thoughts and feelings. Two people who are very dissimilar may act the same way on the outside but feel very differently inside. Take another look at the grid in chapter 4 on page 40. Remember that we have already seen the difficulty in making too many assumptions based on outward behavior. We need to see past the actions to the inner feelings before we can begin to trust our perceptions.

Needs

It wouldn't be so difficult to figure people out if they always stayed in their active behavior, the most effective operating style. But they don't. Any number of things can happen to prevent us from feeling good about ourselves, in which case we tend to step out of our active, most effective behaviors and begin to react more defensively and less productively. This takes place any time our needs are not met.

Needs are the most significant and revealing aspect of our personalities. Needs reflect the basic person—the soul—and when we are misunderstood or criticized, the wound goes deep. Therefore, each need is a mandate, and how that need is handled determines our destinies. Consequently, there is fear associated with expressing our needs. Unfortunately, we often fail to recognize our own needs, much less the underlying needs of others.

Needs are inherited, while the expression of those needs is learned social behavior. An individual's outward behavior may be observed and his stress felt, but there is nothing in the sensory perception that can clue one in on the underlying needs, especially when an individual chooses to hide or suppress them. The deepest needs are the most resistant to change.

In addressing needs, we must first understand and accept them so that healing or behavior modification can take place when appropriate.

Secondly, we need to try to remove some of the fear or stigma that is sometimes attached to the term *needs*. If we think of someone in terms of being "needy," the image may be associated with being poor, homeless, emotionally frail, pathetic, etc. Yet one of the fundamental truths of life is that we all have needs.

For example, we all need vitamin C, a vitamin that promotes rosy cheeks, healthy gums, and resistance to colds. Is this need good . . . or bad, since needing vitamin C suggests that we are weak or lacking in a specific area?

After only a little thought, you should come to the conclusion that your need for vitamin C is neither good nor bad. It is simply a fact of life. Your body needs vitamin C and always will. Your options are either to provide it and maximize your health, or ignore the need and risk the consequences. If you choose to ignore the need, you will catch more colds, your complexion will grow pale, your gums will rot, your teeth will fall out, and you may eventually die of scurvy.

Those who witness your symptoms may want to help you. But they may not know exactly what to do. At one time they might have had a physical ailment of their own and discovered that vitamin A was the cure. Now that you are ill, they may want to relieve your symptoms by giving you large doses of vitamin A, the prescription that cured them.

Such friends mean well, yet their intervention can make your condition even worse. By prescribing the vitamin that was so helpful to them, they prevent you from getting the vitamin C you really need. As a management consultant, I see this kind of behavior all the time. The root of many problems is not that people don't care, but that they're going around giving each other the wrong vitamins!

When your needs for your own "behavioral vitamins" are met, you will react in a positive way because you feel good—optimistic, emotionally healthy, and ready for action. But when those needs are not met, you will feel a significant amount of stress.

Stress

If *active behavior* is the way you act when you're at your best, feeling good, and having your needs met, *reactive behavior* (stress) is what happens when those needs go unfulfilled. Your unmet needs can lead to negative behavior, and your negative behavior can create additional stress and nonproductive results. It's a destructive cycle that continues until you do something about it.

Many things can trigger defensive, reactive behavior. Sometimes the source is a physical illness, fatigue, personal trauma, or excessive and prolonged changes in lifestyle. More commonly, however, the cause of a person's reactive behavior is an actual or perceived inability to have some motivational need met. And one of the biggest problems with reactive behavior is that it frequently spawns similar behavior in other people.

Acts:
    Assertive
    Bossy
    Impatient
Feels:
    Dogmatic
    Narrow-minded
    Resistive

Acts:
    Assertive
    Bossy
    Impatient
Feels:
    Hurt
    Overly sensitive
    Guilty

Acts:
    Submissive
    Withdrawn
    Resigned
Feels:
    Dogmatic
    Narrow-minded
    Resistive

Acts:
    Submissive
    Withdrawn
    Resigned
Feels:
    Hurt
    Overly sensitive
    Guilty

Yet even during times of intense stress, people's actions remain somewhat consistent. And reactive behaviors can be categorized according to the four colors of the Birkman grid. For example, the following chart demonstrates the different ways a person may act and feel when his or her needs are not being met. Notice the differences between the person's outward behavior and actual feelings.

Remember, when motivational needs are being met, we respond with our active or strength behavior. Insofar as we achieve anything, we tend to do it using our active behavior. When we do not have our needs met, the natural tendency is to exhibit corresponding reactive behavior, which is counter-productive and frequently self-defeating. It's important to understand that our need in any area may be quite different from our active behavior.

Again, you can see that the way a person acts does not necessarily reveal the way he or she feels. Nor does it reveal the underlying need. It's never easy to determine a person's feelings based on behavior alone, and this is especially true during intensely stressful times. When needs go unmet, stress or reactive behavior results. In addition, periods of stress may cause observers to jump to conclusions. When people begin to revert to their reactive behaviors, they aren't usually able to evaluate symptoms objectively. They simply become defensive. Consequently, any possibility of effective communication is lost.

Even though you can't determine another person's feelings after he or she has shifted into reactive behavior, it is possible to observe the signs of this kind of behavior in oneself or others. With practice and discipline, these can act as emotional "stop signs" to help us maintain self-control in situations that could very well get out of hand. When you circle your Need color on the following chart, you will be alerted to situations in which your reactive behaviors are likely to surface. Recognizing the need that triggers reactive behavior enables you to choose to stay effective and productive.

The breakdown on page 70 shows some of the more frequent expressions of reactive behavior groups according to the Life Style

Grid variations in attitudes and internal feelings. These outward clues should alert you that the person is not in his or her socialized, active state of behavior.

Your Motivational Needs

The sample breakdown below illustrates some of the needs that trigger reactive behaviors displayed on the following page. To identify your color, review all of the statements below and mark five with which you can identify. Then circle the color of the group with the most marked items. Most people's needs cluster under one color primarily. If you have marked statements under two or more colors, your needs are somewhere in between, and you can draw on the strengths represented by the other colors when meeting your motivational needs.

Needs:
_____ Plenty to do
_____ Clear-cut decisions
_____ Strong supervision
_____ Tangible benefits

Needs:
_____ Discussion and debate
_____ Novelty and change
_____ Competitive relationships
_____ Independent action

Needs:
_____ To know exactly what to do
_____ Scheduled activities
_____ To feel part of the group
_____ Clearly defined authority

Needs:
_____ Freedom from social demands
_____ Time for decisions
_____ Low-key direction
_____ Personal, warm relationships

Reactive Behavior

Under stress becomes:
Unsympathetic
Bossy
Dogmatic
Impulsive
Edgy
Impatient

Under stress becomes:
Defensive
Concerned with saving
    face
Argumentative
Resistant to rules
Easily side-tracked

Under stress becomes:
Too factual
Over-controling
Opinionated
Fearful of the unexpected
Resistant to change

Under stress becomes:
Sensitive to criticism
Easily hurt
Idealistic
Withdrawn
Hesitant to make decisions

As we begin to identify recurring stress (reactive) behavior that reveals the corresponding motivational need in ourselves and others, we can learn to manage our behavior and even deal with the reactive behavior of others. If a manager has a number of people reporting to her, she will do well to recognize the reactive behaviors of those people. (These are likely to vary from person to person.) When she does, she can learn to tell almost immediately when a situation has moved from one of productive interaction to one of stressful, defensive behavior.

Components

In the last chapter dealing with interests, we listed ten specific categories. In this chapter we will deal with eleven other components (esteem, acceptance, structure, authority, advantage, activity, empathy, change, thought, freedom, and challenge) which apply to the three remaining areas of personality: effective style (active behavior), needs, and stress (reactive) behavior.

The following pages describe two colors in each of the summary explanations of typical behavior. The first color listed in each group is the one featured. The second color shares the same motivational need, but to a lesser degree and in somewhat modified form.

I. **Relating to People Individually** (esteem)

This component measures your relationships with other people on a one-to-one basis—husband or wife, boss, and close friends. The **Active** Behavior of this component reflects the way you treat other people. **Need** indicates the way you prefer to be treated. The **Reactive** Behavior shows the way you are likely to behave when this need is not met. *Please keep in mind that since the behavior of the first color listed is the most intense for this component, it is the one featured.*

Red and *Yellow* **Behavior**

Active: You generally deal with others on the basis of frankness, openness, and directness. You feel at ease with superiors. You don't try to hide your feelings, yet you can remain objective and unemotional when dealing with problems and relating to others.

Need: You prefer for others to be open and direct with you. You like for your relationships to have a minimum of sentiment. You don't want people telling you what they think you want to hear.

Reactive: During times of stress, you tend to become insensitive and show a lack of concern for the sensitive feelings of others. You also have difficulty responding to the personal needs of others as you become too factual and abrupt.

Blue and *Green* **Behavior**

Active: You are serious and earnest in your relationships. You have insight into other people's feelings and treat them with respect and appreciation. You also seek the respect of the key people in your life, and you tend to value status.

Need: You prefer for people to show respect and appreciation in their dealings with you. You also prefer that any criticism of you be moderated by an understanding of your personal qualities.

Reactive: During times of stress, you feel ill at ease with superiors and lack emotional toughness. You can become overly sensitive and lose your self-confidence.

Conflicting perceptions of individual relationships: A Red person sees a Blue person as overly sensitive and a dreamer.

A Blue person sees a Red person as blunt and insensitive.

II. **Relating to People in Groups** (acceptance)

Relating to people on a broader basis tends to be more casual than relationships with individuals. **Active** Behavior shows how you relate to other people on this basis. **Need** shows how you prefer to be treated with regard to groups. **Reactive** Behavior shows the way you are likely to behave when this need is not met. *Please keep in mind that since the behavior of the first color listed is the most intense for this component, it is the one featured.*

Yellow and *Red* Behavior

Active: You enjoy teamwork and work well with groups. You enjoy meeting people, are socially adaptive, and get along well with people as a whole. Sometimes, however, you tend to be agreeable merely for the sake of staying on someone's "good side."

Need: You need the support of a group. It is important to you to feel that you are accepted by people and that you are in control. At times, you take strong stands for the feeling of security it offers.

Reactive: During times of stress, you tend to tell others what you think they want to hear. You may be easily swayed by others' opinions. Even though you can have many friends, you are likely to avoid close personal relationships.

Blue and *Green* Behavior

Active: You like to work and think independently of the group. You don't work well when forced into group decisions or committee work. You prefer tasks that involve your working alone or among those with whom you are fairly close.

Need: You need to be allowed to spend a significant amount of time on your own or with close friends or associates. You don't like having to interact with people on a casual basis. You are able to withstand the pressure of group opinion and work alone.

Reactive: During times of stress, you may get impatient with other people and ignore them. You tend to withdraw and underestimate the importance of groups.

Conflicting perceptions of group relationships: A Yellow Person sees a Blue person as withdrawn and antisocial.

A Blue person sees a Yellow person as a follower, a popularity-seeker, or a yes-man.

III. **Systems and Procedures** (structure)

This component measures the way you prefer to relate to systems and procedures. The most comfortable levels of structured detail and order vary from person to person. **Active** Behavior reflects the extent to which you tend to impose system and order on both your own activities and the activities of others. **Need** shows how you need to be treated by others. **Reactive** Behavior shows the way you are likely to behave when this need is not met. *Please keep in mind that* *since the behavior of the first color listed is the most intense for this component, it is the one featured.*

Yellow and *Red* **Behavior**

Active: You have a concern for detail and the ability to impose system upon your activities. You prefer working to a predetermined plan. You like both stability and predictability in your jobs. Your ability to organize and follow through on your tasks is a considerable asset as long as you don't develop an overly rigid insistence on following precedent and procedure.

Need: You need a structured schedule, plan, and environment. You need a list of things to do and the order in which they are to be done. You also want the support of the organization in whatever you do. You need to structure your own approach to certain tasks, but you prefer to have a larger organizational plan to work by.

Reactive: During times of stress, you begin to fear the unknown and become security-minded. You resist change and may tend to overcontrol the things you are working on. You lose morale when pressured and revert to previously established procedures. Most Yellows tend to be more salary- than commission-oriented.

Blue and *Green* **Behavior**

Active: Your approach to tasks is characterized by flexibility, an enjoyment of novelty, and a readiness to try out new methods of solving problems. You're unusually motivated to try out new things and accept new assignments. Your ability to think outside of established procedures may make you a good planner, though you may sometimes tend to play down the value of precedent or working according to an established plan.

Need: You need broad control exercised over you. You welcome opportunities for personal initiative and a minimum of routine. You don't do well under closely supervised conditions. You would rather be given the "big picture" and then left to work out the details on your own.

Reactive: During times of stress, you ignore necessary routines and follow-through, become rebellious toward authority, or tend to over-generalize. You tend to leave things to the last minute or lose interest and begin to neglect important details.

Conflicting perceptions of structured environments: A Yellow person sees a Blue person as disorganized and impractical.

A Blue person sees a Yellow person as unimaginative, procedural, and by-the-book.

IV. **Authority Relationships** (control)

Authority relationships define the way you relate to direction and control and measure the need to direct others or be directed. While Structure deals more with written or otherwise established procedures, Authority involves more of an interpersonal element. The **Active** Behavior score tells how you exercise control in your dealings with other people. **Need** indicates the kind of environment you prefer with regard to the exercise of direction and control. **Reactive** Behavior shows the way you are likely to behave when this need is not met. *Please keep in mind that since the behavior of the first color listed is the most intense for this component, it is the one featured.*

Green and *Red* **Behavior**

Active: You are self-assertive. You enjoy directing the activities of others and are quite prepared to argue a point if you find yourself in disagreement. You like to take stands on issues. You have a capacity to be outspoken and to the point, and you leave no doubt as to who is in control. You seek to excel, to influence others, and are probably quite competitive.

Need: You need to sense strong control from your superiors. Your environment should offer the assurance of well-defined boundaries and firm direction by the appropriate authority figures and opportunities for forthright discussion of policies and decisions. You want strong, face-to-face supervision.

Reactive: During times of stress, you become bossy, domineering, and demand special attention. You tend to express your opinions too freely and act provocatively. You enjoy open disagreement and arguments.

Blue and *Yellow* Behavior

Active: You prefer to exercise your authority in an atmosphere of pleasant and controlled relationships. You probably ask people to do things rather than order them. You are self-directive, independent, anxious to please, and you try to avoid open clashes. Your agreeable approach probably works well for you, though in some difficult situations, you may have an undue reluctance to be firm.

Need: You need pleasant and protective relationships. You also need the broad control of the system and a title to back up your authority. When complaints are made, you prefer not to handle them yourself and usually look to someone else to deal with them.

Reactive: During times of stress, you have trouble speaking up and asserting yourself apart from formal, assigned authority. You try to avoid disagreement. You are uncomfortable actively directing others, and you resist authoritarian management.

Conflicting perceptions of authority relationships: A Green person sees a Blue person as weak and submissive.

A Blue person sees a Green person as pushy and domineering.

V. **Teamwork and Individual Competition** (advantage)

This category has something of a dual definition. On the one hand, it refers to the amount of competition you need—how individually competitive you are. But closely related to this is the area of materialism. Some people thrive on individual achievement and the tangible symbols that reward personal accomplishment—raises, company cars, prestigious offices, etc. Others have a more altruistic, team-oriented and trusting approach to their tasks. In this category, **Active** Behavior is an indication of the way you behave with regard to competition. **Need** shows the environment you prefer and the way you like to be treated by others. **Reactive** Behavior shows the way you are likely to behave when this need is not met. *Please keep in mind that since the behavior of the first color listed is the most intense for this component, it is the one featured.*

Red and *Green* Behavior

Active: You are personally competitive and like to be recognized for what you do. You enjoy promotional and money-making ventures. Opportunity-minded, you are resourceful in your dealings with others. You have a strong drive for income and may have a low regard for, or even a suspicion of, other people as being too idealistic, impractical, and unrealistic.

Need: You need concrete, tangible rewards as recognition of your individual merit. Your environment should be competitively oriented with an emphasis on individual ability. You want immediate rewards for accomplishments as well as special reassurance concerning personal advancement.

Reactive: During times of stress, you think and act to protect your self-interests, placing too much importance on personal advantage and self-protection. You can become distrustful and opportunistic.

Yellow and *Blue* Behavior

Active: You place an emphasis on the long-term values of your work. Trust and consistency are dominant features of your approach. You are motivated by maintaining the integrity of your job. You keep in mind the well-being of others as well as the long-term benefits of what you're doing.

Need: You need to measure your work in terms of purpose as well as reward. Your environment should stress the usefulness of your work and should encourage teamwork and loyalty. You appreciate opportunities to help others and assignments that minimize competitive rivalry.

Reactive: During times of stress, you can become unrealistic as you tend to underestimate other people's self-serving traits and allow others to take advantage of you. If placed in a position of having to bargain for something, you become very uncomfortable and impractical.

Conflicting perceptions of personal advantage: A Red person sees a Yellow person as impractical and idealistic.

A Yellow person sees a Red person as materialistic, opportunistic, and willing to take advantage of others to get what he or she wants.

VI. **Action- or Reflection-Oriented Approach** (activity)

This component refers to the amount of physical (as opposed to reflective) activity that characterizes your work and play. It also indicates the approach you take to dealing with problems that arise. **Active** Behavior indicates your preferred, most productive behavior. **Need** shows the kind of environment you need and the way you need to be treated by others. **Reactive** Behavior shows the way you are likely to behave when this need is not met. *Please keep in mind that since the behavior of the first color listed is the most intense in the component, it is the one featured.*

Red and *Green* **Behavior**

Active: You have a high energy level and it is important for you to be active for a large part of your day. You have the stamina to accommodate a demanding schedule. You can handle (and probably enjoy) lots of work.

Need: You need a variety of tasks that will keep you busy and active. You may need help restraining your enthusiasm and plenty of opportunities to blow off steam. You may not be able to exert all your energy in a work setting, and will need to find social outlets as well.

Reactive: During times of stress, you tend to waste a lot of energy by acting without thinking. You become impatient and reluctant to change your ideas. You can become edgy and impatient, and have trouble delegating.

Blue and *Yellow* Behavior

Active: You prefer a reflection-oriented approach that makes the best use of your energy. You prefer to think through problems before "diving in" to try to solve them. You prefer not to move too hastily or run all day. You try to learn something from everyone and are probably a good delegator.

Need: You need an environment that permits a certain amount of time for making decisions and for thought, one that does not place the demands of a heavy schedule on you. You prefer a live-and-let-live atmosphere and the opportunity to set your own pace.

Reactive: During times of stress, you get bored easily. As a result, you are likely to put things off and become easily discouraged. As you delay taking necessary action, you tend to lose competitive energy.

Conflicting perceptions of preferred activity levels: A Red person sees a Blue person as lazy and ineffective.

A Blue person sees a Red person as restless, impatient, and busy for the sake of being busy.

VII. **Objectivity and Subjectivity** (empathy)

This component measures the extent to which feelings are part of your makeup and the degree to which you see emotion as a significant factor in your dealings with other people. **Active** Behavior shows to what extent you display feelings in your relationships. **Need** indicates how much you want others to take your feelings into account. **Reactive** Behavior shows the way you are likely to behave when this need is not met. *Please keep in mind that since the behavior of the first color listed is the most intense for this component, it is the one featured.*

Red and *Yellow* Behavior

Active: You are detached, factual, and objective in your relationships and do not allow your emotions to cloud the issues. You are logical and seek practical results. Because you hold definite opinions, you may occasionally overlook important emotional elements in your dealings with others.

Need: You need to be treated in a matter-of-fact manner since you prefer not to deal with emotional reactions or lots of attention from others. Your environment should offer detached supervision and straightforward instruction. You prefer logical approaches to situations, not personal feelings or high emotions.

Reactive: During times of stress, your feelings may become impersonal and demanding. You tend to minimize problems and place emphasis on immediate results. In the process, you may lose sensitivity toward other people.

Green and *Blue* Behavior

Active: You enjoy warm, genuine relationships, and you are insightful and sympathetic to the feelings of others. People can tell you are caring and involved. You set high expectations that may sometimes be based on immeasurable results. Your high level of sensitivity can make you prone to wide changes of mood.

Need: You need an environment where people are aware of your personal feelings. You want the opportunity to share concepts with them and sell them on your ideas and your friendship. You need special opportunities to confide and probe your inner feelings. Unexpected changes in relationships are likely to make you uncomfortable.

Reactive: During times of stress, you can get very "down" and become too subjective with your feelings and outlook. You dwell on the difficulties in every situation as you lean toward self-pity.

Conflicting perceptions of emotional involvement: A Red person sees a Green person as excessively emotional and moody.

A Green person sees a Red person as impersonal and unfeeling.

VIII. **Handling Varied Assignments** (change)

This component is simply the measure of the extent to which you like change and variety in your life. **Active** Behavior is the amount of change you introduce into your own schedule or the schedules of others. **Need** reflects the amount of change you need to have imposed upon you by your environment or by other people. **Reactive** Behavior shows the way you are likely to behave when this need is not met. *Please keep in mind that since the behavior of the first color listed is the most intense for this component, it is the one featured.*

Green and *Blue* **Behavior**

Active: You enjoy introducing change into your personal affairs and are not averse to bringing similar change to the routines of other people. You also tend to enjoy taking on a wide assortment of tasks. You thrive on variety and novelty. A new schedule every day is fine with you. You will get bored if you must maintain a regular, rigid schedule. But you need to avoid introducing change for its own sake when it is not really required.

Need: You need the opportunity for varied—even unconventional— work situations and changes in activity. You also need new challenges or special projects to compensate for your tendency to get bored easily. The more new and different projects you are allowed to do, the better you will feel about your work.

Reactive: During times of stress, you will have trouble concentrating on issues and may have a hard time sitting still. Self-discipline will not come easily. You will be annoyed by delays and are likely to be excitable.

Yellow and *Red* Behavior

Active: You are likely to try to keep change to a minimum. You are probably able to concentrate on a given project for a sustained period of time during which you resist distractions. You show dedication to the job at hand and generally deal with things as they are. You are consistent, thorough, and prefer to complete one project before starting another.

Need: You need to have a minimum of change imposed on you. You crave the support of an environment that permits concentration on one task at a time. And you want others to respect your ability to see the overall picture and stick to a procedure or a system you are familiar with. When change is imminent, you need time to anticipate and prepare for it.

Reactive: During times of stress, you tend to over-concentrate and lose perspective. You are also likely to resist abrupt changes and become inflexible in your thinking and attitude.

Conflicting perspectives of dealing with change: A Green person sees a Yellow person as unadventurous and resistant to change.

A Yellow person sees a Green person as restless, lacking self-discipline, and wanting change for the sake of change.

IX. **Making Decisions** (thought)

This component is a measure of the length of time it takes to make a decision—only the time it takes to decide, not the quality of the decision. **Active** Behavior is the length of time it usually takes you to make a routine decision (compared to how long it takes other people). **Need** is an indication of the amount of time you like to be given in decision-making. It also tells you how long you tend to take when making decisions that require a consideration of unusual or unique factors. **Reactive** Behavior shows the way you are likely to behave when this need is not met. *Please keep in mind that since the behavior of the first color listed is the most intense for this component, it is the one featured.*

Red and *Yellow* Behavior

Active: You tend to make decisions rapidly and in an objective, matter-of-fact manner. You grasp situations and weigh competing factors quickly, and you don't take long to form judgments. You enjoy being logical and decisive, but you can occasionally be impetuous.

Need: You need opportunities to take decisive action, so you want definite and decisive supervision. You don't need a lot of time to make a decision and are capable of rapid, decisive action—even under pressure. But you need for situations to be presented to you in clear, unambiguous terms.

Reactive: During times of stress, you tend to become frustrated with ambiguity and make decisions too hastily. You can also lose sight of the long-term implications of your decisions and react impulsively.

Blue and *Green* Behavior

Active: Since you have the ability to see all sides of an issue, you take longer to reach a decision. You also like to get the input of others before committing yourself. You are able to take into account the consequences of your decisions and have a natural tendency to root out all relevant considerations in your decision-making. In your resistance to acting too quickly, you sometimes tend to delay too long in taking action.

Need: You need to feel that you have plenty of time to make up your mind. You also want assurance that advice is available from other people. Especially in pressure situations, you need to be reassured that you are making the right decision.

Reactive: During times of stress, you tend to worry and become afraid of making mistakes. You become uncertain and begin to procrastinate.

Conflicting perceptions of decision-making style: A Red person sees a Blue person as indecisive, delaying, and obstructive.

A Blue person sees a Red person as overly simplistic, impetuous, and impulsive—too quick on the draw.

X. **Personal Independence** (freedom)

Freedom is a measure of the extent to which you need to be out from under social constraints. It reflects the degree to which you feel and demonstrate your individuality; it is essentially the opposite of conformity. **Active** Behavior tells you to what extent you choose to behave as an individual. **Need** indicates how you like to be treated by other people or the kind of environment you prefer. **Reactive** Behavior shows the way you are likely to behave when this need is not met. *Please keep in mind that since the behavior of the first color listed is the most intense for this component, it is the one featured.*

Green **and** *Blue* **Behavior**

Active: You feel you are rather different from most people. Your behavior is more distinctive and individualistic, and you will not necessarily be bound by convention. You don't regard precedent as a limitation for trying new ideas and approaches, and you probably appreciate the value of an unusual solution to a difficult situation. You may need to be careful not to espouse unconventional notions merely because they are different.

Need: Your surroundings should offer plenty of opportunity for self-expression and self-determination. You need to be free to set your own goals and standards.

Reactive: During times of stress, you may become a nonconformist to the point of being rebellious. You get a bit too individualistic at times and misjudge the "average" person.

Yellow and *Red* Behavior

Active: You tend to regard yourself as very much the same as other people and want to fit in with the others on the team. Your behavior is consistent and restrained, and you are fairly conventional in attitude. You usually understand the thoughts and attitudes of the average person, and you are likely to dismiss most unconventional ideas as a waste of time.

Need: You need order in your life. You need a predictable environment that offers the reassurance of consistency and predictability.

Reactive: During times of stress, you can become anxious and nervous and are likely to repress your inner feelings. You may seem inhibited and you dread the unexpected.

Conflicting perceptions of personal freedom: A Green person sees a Yellow person as dull and conventional.

A Yellow person sees a Green person as unpredictable and intolerant of any constraints on his or her freedom, regardless of the needs of society.

XI. **Self-Image** (challenge)

Any Color

The self-image component is unique. This becomes a measure of how you relate to the demands of your work or of any project you are involved in. In essence, it is a measure of self-image and can to some extent be used as a measure of self-confidence as well. This self-image component infuses all of your perceptions and expectations and relates directly to all the other components and colors.

Positive Self-Image

Active: You are reasonable in your expectations of yourself and others. You have confidence in your abilities. You have a track record of success and want to extend it. You are probably persuasive, charming, and can express your feelings easily. You also tend to choose tasks that you know are within your capabilities. Sometimes you have an inability to accept any criticism of yourself.

Need: You need to feel that your goals and plans are reasonable, even if they are demanding. You want to see the potential for success for yourself and others. You probably need to be involved in some kind of socially challenging and service-type activities.

Reactive: During times of stress, you may get carried away with your own enthusiasm and/or blame things on others. When faced with strong opposition, you lose emotional strength. You tend to follow the path of least emotional resistance and you avoid introspection and self-examination.

Self-Critical Image

Active: You take pride in your own achievements, yet you're frequently critical of your performance and that of others. You may feel responsible for problems in which you are not even involved. Though you are aware of personal shortcomings, you seek demanding challenges. You are strong-willed and critical in your analysis of problems and performance.

Need: You need difficult and demanding goals. You need to feel that tasks require the very most from you, even at the risk of failure. You want to take on tasks that can be done well, and you appreciate strong and fair supervision.

Reactive: During times of stress, you're too tough on yourself and tend to take the blame unnecessarily. Your performance becomes erratic and you feel inadequate. You can be unconsciously defiant in subtle ways, and you may even sabotage your own efforts due to fear of failure.

Conflicting perceptions: A Positive Self-Image person sees a Self-Critical person as too self-critical, demanding, and unsure of self.

A Self-Critical person sees a person with a Positive Self-Image as too self-confident, too quick to blame others, and self-aggrandizing.

In Summary

Identifying your own combination of components and the components that make up the *True Colors* of others is an ongoing challenge. But no doubt you have identified specific areas that describe your distinctive personality.

The complexity of all eleven components is a great deal to take in in one sitting. But I hope you see how much is involved in the exploration of personality and behavior, and have begun to understand why it is so important to identify the motivations distributed within and among the colors and the various ways we respond to them.

Most existing personality evaluations group together the person's behaviors and omit the motivational needs. But it is revealing when we break them down and deal with them separately. Surely it makes sense to see that though you usually behave in a certain way in some areas, you have vastly different needs.

CHAPTER 7

HEALING OLD WOUNDS

Anyone who has been around very long at all has lots of stories to tell. Some may be written in books or recorded on tape. Others may live only in the memory. Still others are triggered by visible reminders that remain on the body in the form of scars from injuries or accidents.

• "See this scar on my toe? I dropped a chisel on it and almost cut it off when I was six."

• "I got this one when I walked through a glass door when I was a teenager."

• "This one's from sliding headfirst into second base in that rocky Texas soil when I was a kid."

You may carry scars from a dog bite, an operation, or a smallpox vaccination. But the most painful scars are often those you can't see, those that lie buried in the subconscious. Perhaps those wounds are still open, continuing to fester long after the initial injury. And since no visible scars exist for those emotional wounds, other people may touch the sore places unknowingly and cause severe discomfort.

Many of these emotional wounds are based on our own self-perceptions. We may see ourselves in a certain way that is completely off-base. And until we address the misperceptions, the pain will continue. In this chapter we will deal with trying to correct improper self-perceptions.

The Things We've Been Told

As you read through the components of behavior in the last chapter, I hope you discovered that no matter where a person finds himself on the scale, the characteristics are positive. If a person is true to his or her unique strengths, it's not "right" to be one way and "wrong" to be another. And while one person's characteristics can be just about as different as possible from another person's, both of them can be equally right. Yet many of us continue to struggle with what we *aren't* rather than being satisfied with what we *are*.

Our problems usually begin externally. Other people make observations about us that may be well-intentioned, yet completely wrong. At first their comments may not sink in. But one day a remark strikes hard enough to break the emotional skin. Maybe we forget about it and the wound begins to heal. But before the healing is complete, another remark comes along. Then another. And another. And before we know it, we have an open wound. The pain it causes affects us more than we know. Our attitudes, behaviors, and decisions are all influenced by the pain and by our desperate desire not to do anything to worsen it.

The best thing to do at such times is to be completely honest with ourselves. The truth is always the best cure for emotional wounds. But we've been taught that "the truth hurts," so we resist getting down to the root of the matter. Yet if we could convince ourselves of the truths covered in chapter 3 of this book, we could stitch up our open wounds and let them begin to heal.

Let's look at a few of the things you may have heard from other people and see how their comments stack up against the truth. Even if you've heard these things from people you trust—parents, teachers, close friends—it is in your best interest to examine them objectively and see if you truly believe what you've been told.

"You should be like . . ."

- "Your father was the best businessman I ever knew. You couldn't do better than to pattern your life after his."

- "Since we're best friends and I want to be a lawyer, why don't you go to law school too, and we can be partners when we graduate?"

- "You've done well in my history class. You should consider being a teacher like me."

We all hear comments like these. People see us in one particular area and make bold recommendations based on their perceptions. In most cases they probably mean well and genuinely want to help. (It should go without saying, however, that some people will try to influence you out of less than pure motives—jealousy, to make a sale, to get you riled up just for the fun of it, etc.)

Yet even the most well-intentioned people can only observe you from the outside. They may not be able to read your inner thoughts, feelings, attitudes, interests, hopes, dreams, and needs. And in trying to help, they might steer you down a path that is completely wrong for you. Some families have four or five generations of descendants who have attended the same college, gone into the same vocation, and established a tradition that is expected of everyone else who follows. And while I can't say for sure that this would be *wrong* for the next young person to go down the same path, I don't think anyone else can say for sure that it's *right*.

I think this is one reason we see so many midlife career adjustments. People who have spent twenty years trying to be someone else get to the point where they say, "I've had enough, and I can't take it anymore." Some take bold steps to change. They drop out of the "rat race" and, for the first time in their lives, begin to think about what they would really enjoy doing.

In addition, the past few years have seen a boom of entrepreneurial enterprises. Fewer people are automatically going into "big business."

Instead, they are finding their own creative niche and are learning how to make a living using their specific skills and interests.

We can all learn much from the personal heroes in our lives, but we may be in for a long period of confusion and grief if we try to become just like someone else. The truth of the matter is that each of us is special and unique. And until we identify that uniqueness and find out how we're different (rather than "just like" someone else), we aren't likely to be happy.

"You should be a . . ."

- "You're good in science. You should be a doctor."

- "Look at all of Johnny's drawings on the refrigerator. I think he's going to be a great artist."

- "Here's a list of the '100 Top-Paying Jobs.' Pick one and choose a major that will help you get there."

In addition to getting advice on *whom* we should emulate, many of us are also advised about exactly *what* we should become. Sometimes very little effort is put into the advice that is offered. Perhaps the son of a coworker is a success in his career. Or maybe a television actor makes that career look interesting. That's all some people need to advise their own children to pursue that field.

At other times bosses become more concerned with filling job openings with "warm bodies" than in finding good matches for an employee's skills. For example, one publishing company had a manager who was the ultimate "people person." His job was to work with authors, acquire manuscripts, and train in-house people. Not only was he good at what he did, but he was also the company's best morale-builder. He was a bundle of energy, seldom walking when he could run and usually whistling, clapping, laughing, and otherwise motivating others.

When the company decided to produce its first Bible—a labor-intensive project that included hundreds of illustrations and study helps interspersed throughout the text—the top executives put this person in charge because he was so easy to get along with. The thought of heading up such a worthwhile project was appealing to the guy as well. But gradually his job description changed dramatically. Financial margins were tight, so upper management didn't hire a staff to work with him. Instead, he had to deal with freelancers over the phone. Nor were his previous job responsibilities sufficiently revised to give him adequate time to devote to his new project.

Soon the project he had taken on with the best of intentions had become a real headache. With no previous corporate experience in Bible publishing, every problem that came up was left for this one guy to handle. In addition, he was doing the actual desktop publishing, so more and more of his days were spent in front of a computer terminal. He no longer had time to work with authors or train the people who reported to him. And since this person was the only one who really knew what was going on, he was pretty much left in charge of the marketing and promotion as well, all while trying to complete the project!

Before it was all over, the man was sleeping on the floor of his office a couple of hours each night, devoting literally every waking moment to the project. Even contact with his wife and kids had all but disappeared. Meanwhile, upper management did nothing to relieve the killing pace of his schedule, much less address his real interests.

Not surprisingly, the project didn't turn out to be the immense success that company executives had hoped for. But rather than returning to what had worked well before, they refused to give up on Bible publishing. And since the only person who knew anything about it was the guy who had worked on the first one, his job description completely changed, with little hope of returning to the responsibilities he had originally enjoyed.

Fortunately, someone who *could* clearly see the man's strengths made him an offer to teach in a local college. That's what he's been doing for the past several years, and loving every minute of it. He still takes on some publishing projects on the side—working with authors and doing the "people" things he has always loved to do. Now that his career is based on his strengths and interests—working with people—he couldn't be happier. Meanwhile, the division of the company where he was employed has had an almost complete turn-over of employees, and their low morale is no secret in the industry.

Sometimes it's difficult for older, more experienced adults to detect the subtle shifts that move them away from their unique strengths. So it should come as no surprise that young people are particularly vulnerable to advice that encourages them to pursue some specific vocation or interest. Few of us as teenagers knew what we wanted to do with the rest of our lives. Yet it is precisely at this uncertain age that we are called upon to determine where we're going to college, what our major will be, and what part-time jobs we will take. Needing advice, we welcome the counsel of trusted friends and family members. Yet we need to be sure not to put too much stock in the advice of others if it conflicts with our own instincts as to what would be best for us. One of our top consultants learned this firsthand. "I always assumed my daughter was like me," she says, "with a high need for Freedom and a low need for Structure [referring to the components detailed in the last chapter]. But during all our time together we had been at odds. I even sent her to school in Europe, thinking it would be as terrific for her as *I* thought it would be for me. But all she wanted to do was come home. I eventually discovered she was just my opposite in the areas of Freedom and Structure. I also found out that the Golden Rule doesn't always apply: If we do unto others as we want them to do to us, we may miss some of their specific needs."

"Here's the secret to success."

Most people are full of advice based on their own personal experience. Such advice should be received with caution. As you begin to recognize variations in personality, you also become aware that what works for one person won't necessarily work for another.

Suppose you're reading a book on time management by an author who has a high Active Behavior score in the Activity component. Such a person would tend to be doing something all the time. His or her advice would probably include a lot of little activities that other people would consider a waste of time: "Make a list of everything you have to do. Number the things on your list in order of priority. Do Item #1 first. When you finish, check off that activity from your list."

There's nothing wrong with such advice. But a "low-activity" person would prefer to think through the activities that must be done and put more energy into the tasks themselves rather than in organizing, categorizing, and otherwise evaluating the tasks.

People who don't understand this, however, are at the mercy of those who sell solutions for every problem. Many of them go through life trying to practice various authors' techniques for making more money, losing weight, increasing sales, being a better parent, and on and on. When the advice doesn't work, they tend to blame themselves: *What am I doing wrong?* they wonder. *If it worked so well for him, why isn't it working for me?*

It doesn't work because each person is a unique and special individual. And the only lasting secret to success is discovering who you really are and developing your own strategies!

Things We Tell Ourselves

The previous examples have all been based on external comments—the things we are told by other people. That's usually where the problems begin. But if such comments go unchecked, we can develop even worse problems. We may begin to tell *ourselves* things that are negative and destructive. Following are some of the common self-perceptions that can hurt us if we don't identify and eliminate them:

"I just need to work harder and everything will be all right."

There is certainly nothing wrong with hard work, though it is not a panacea for all our problems. Many of us have been brought up with the subliminal, if not the outright, perception that work is good, rest is bad. We hear:

• "Idle hands are the devil's workshop."

• "Man may work from sun to sun, but woman's work is never done."

• "There is no substitute for hard work. . . . Genius is one percent inspiration and ninety-nine percent perspiration" (Thomas Edison).

Oh, sure, we also hear: "All work and no play makes Jack a dull boy." But most of us figure that if Jack's long hours make him rich, dullness is a side-effect he can live with!

Workaholic tendencies are common today—in our personal endeavors as well as on the job. Some of us have never learned to determine when we've done enough and when it's time to take a well-deserved rest. And while most people agree that this is a problem, it seems that few victims of workaholism can manage to do what is necessary to change.

At the root of the problem is the same issue we've already discussed—an unspoken, unwritten standard of what is "normal." Someone who is devoted to the job or wants to "get ahead" is a person who is at work before everyone else and is still there when the others go home. He or she can talk on the phone all day while simultaneously handling correspondence, planning, and taking care of any emergencies that come up. Every quarter this person manages to come in ahead of schedule and under budget. Bosses smile at this person and pat him or her on the back at every opportunity. This person is an excellent public speaker, knows all the latest jokes (politically correct ones, of course), and has a portrait of spouse and family hanging in the office, suggesting a home life that is equally as idyllic as his life at work. (Of course, the portrait is probably there to remind the person what the spouse and family look like—in lieu of any personal contact!)

And even people who do manage to make time for family, church, and other activities in addition to work may not be as ideal as they appear to be. While such a lifestyle may be fine for some people, it certainly shouldn't be assumed that it's best for everyone. As you should have seen in the discussion of the Activity component in the last chapter, there is no direct correlation between activity and efficiency. Some people are much more efficient when sitting still and thinking through a plan of action than when maintaining a perpetually hectic pace.

There is no single standard for the *best* way to work. Your way— the method that is most natural and comfortable in regard to your specific personality components—will probably accomplish more than if you try to work according to someone else's design. You can work long and hard, but if you are continually "going against the grain" of your personal strengths, you will probably face perpetual frustration on the job. No amount of additional hours will compensate for trying to work according to someone else's standards.

"I have to be perfect."

If workaholism is one major problem, perfectionism is another. Though none of us truly believes we have the capacity for perfection, we may frequently act as if we have such expectations. Every little failure looms large in our perception, blocking out the view of all the good and productive things we have accomplished.

When we put in a few extra hours at work, we feel guilty for not spending enough time with spouse and children. When we take off early to go to a school function for one of the kids, we're preoccupied with all the work we're not getting done. Weekends are always too short for all we had hoped to accomplish. New opportunities seem endless, and we are devastated when we can't pursue them all. The lawn is never quite as manicured as it *should* be. Birthdays cease to be celebrations and become times for performance evaluations. ("I should have gotten a lot more done last year.")

Even though we know perfection is out of the question, many of us just can't seem to be satisfied with less. Consequently, the people we live and work with are usually subject to the same set of criteria we establish for ourselves. It becomes very difficult for others to interact with us when they know nothing they do is ever good enough.

Improving oneself is a fine and noble goal. But when the challenge for improvement turns into an obsession for perfection, deep emotional wounds are formed. The personal lack of fulfillment is a source of ongoing pain, and that pain spreads to others as we pass along our excessively high expectations. It's especially tragic when our perfectionistic tendencies do not allow for any lapse of performance and force us to live by an impossible standard, which brings us to the next consideration.

"I'm such a failure."

At the other end of the spectrum are those who may have already given up on themselves. Somewhere along the way, they have picked up on too many wrong signals and have come to perceive themselves as worthless. Again, this problem is probably due to the fact that they assume one specific standard is "normal"—a standard which they just aren't able to meet.

In the meantime, of course, they have learned to overlook every good and unique thing about themselves. Perhaps no one ever tried to build them up, and they were simply unable to do it themselves. Or perhaps they received so much criticism from family and peers that their self-image was irreparably damaged.

It's not hard to see where this defeatist attitude comes from in our society. Young boys try to model themselves after professional sports figures. Adolescent girls compare their bodies to those of supermodels. The standards they use for self-image are not at all normal, yet no one may be providing them with more realistic standards and affirmation for who they *are* rather than who they aren't. Add to this problem the issue of teasing and verbal cruelty among peers at that age and it's no surprise that many people begin life feeling substandard. If they then experience a failure or two as young adults (which, of course, everyone does), they may start telling *themselves* that they are worthless.

At the heart of the Birkman philosophy is the conviction that everyone has specific strengths. Each person has a set of interests, behaviors, and needs that are appropriate for him or her. And no one who understands and applies those strengths can ever be classified as a "failure." No, not everyone will be a professional athlete, a cover-girl model, or a rocket scientist. If those are the only standards worth shooting for, then more than 99 percent of the world's population are failures.

But just as you can't possibly be someone else, neither can someone else be *you*. So the only criterion of success one should use is whether or not you're becoming the person that only you can be.

Stitching Up Old Wounds

If you've convinced yourself that any of the previous statements are true, or if you've been influenced by others to believe them, you may have some deep emotional wounds.

When treating emotional wounds, it may seem that the remedy is worse than the injury. If you've ever had a tooth filled without Novocaine, you can probably relate to this. You know that it's important for the dentist to drill out all of the decay. If not, the tooth will eventually cause trouble or be lost altogether. Yet the occasional contact of the dentist's instruments with your exposed nerve can take you to previously unimagined levels of pain! When it's over, the tooth is as good as new. But for a while, you may wish you'd left well enough alone.

I urge you to brace yourself and deal with any emotional wounds you are carrying. You may begin to realize that people you trusted have misled you. You may need to come to grips with the fact that a goal you have been desperately pursuing may never be attained. You may learn that you've been spinning your wheels for years in an area that is not going to provide the rewards you had hoped. And all these discoveries will be painful.

But this kind of pain is temporary. From that point on, you can count on the pain to be diminished and health to be restored. So when you're ready, here are some steps to take to close up some of the old wounds.

Step #1: Recognize your uniqueness.

Much of your life to this point may have been spent in trying to determine where you fit in. There's nothing wrong with that. We all like to feel that we belong. The problem arises when we try to force ourselves to belong when we shouldn't: A too-small boy insisting on going out for football to prove that he's as "worthy" as the other guys. A young girl becoming bulimic to avoid being perceived as "fat." An adult choosing to clone herself to a boss's standards and jumping on the success track of long hours and endless devotion to work.

At times it's more important for us to determine exactly where we *don't* fit, to find the places where we stand out. Those are the areas where our unique talents and abilities are going to lie. Of course, as a management consultant, I highly recommend that you consider professional testing to determine your one-of-a-kind combination of strengths. But you can do a lot on your own through trial and error.

For example, you can probably think of certain situations where you always seem to be in the minority. That doesn't necessarily mean you're wrong. In fact, it may mean that you have an idea that no one else can comprehend. Historically, it hasn't been the people in the majority who have changed things for the better. The inventors, explorers, philosophers, theologians, and such have been those who flew boldly in the face of conventional thinking.

The first major step in healing emotional wounds is changing your perception about your natural way of thinking. Don't think of minority thinking as wrong. Think of it as *yours*—uniquely yours. It may very well be that you see something that nobody else is able to see. You don't have to convince anyone that you're right. It's enough for *you* to recognize that you have a different slant on the issue. You can even choose to go along with the crowd in many instances, but you'll know that your own view of the situation is broader (and perhaps even better) than the chosen course of action.

This sounds like a simple step. But if you've spent years trying to fit in with the rest of the crowd, it will probably take a lot of practice to become yourself again. It is essential that you begin by making an effort to find out what you do well and how you differ from most other people in your approach to conflict, relationships, work, and so forth.

Step #2: Get excited about your uniqueness.

As you begin to identify the things that make you a unique individual, you should develop a sense of wonder and adventure. If you've always fought off the impulse to "be your own person" in order to conform to the standards of others, this sensation should feel something like a second childhood. You'll no doubt go though periods of confusion and self-doubt, but eventually you'll begin to catch a fresh vision of the real you.

Your initial transformation from "dependent conformist" to "independent, one-of-a-kind individual" will probably be an inner and gradual shift of perception. You should begin to see your unique attitudes and behaviors as potential benefits rather than absolute shortcomings. But with time, your transformation should become more external and public as well.

You might even surprise yourself someday by saying, "I disagree with that." It really doesn't matter what you're disagreeing with. But the ability to see more than one response to a situation *and the willingness to take a minority stand for what you believe* is a source of great confidence and excitement. People may not always agree with you, but you're more likely to earn their respect than when you kowtow to their every opinion, whether or not you agree.

You'll also discover that using your unique strengths will provide creative answers to problems that no one else will think of. One of the most fascinating consequences of having an infinite variety of people is that everyone brings a different perspective to any problem, discussion, or brainstorming session. When we cave in to a "group-think" mentality, life can get pretty stagnant. But as you get more comfortable with your one-of-a-kind personality and your own brand of personal creativity, life takes on a whole new dimension. All that's left for you to do is unleash it.

Step #3: Practice your uniqueness.

First, you recognize your uniqueness and learn exactly what it is that makes you different from the rest of the world. Next, you dwell on those distinctives until you get excited about who you are. Then it's time to practice, practice, practice. Knowing how you're different can help ease the pain of long-standing wounds, but your ultimate goal should be to actually move on and seek out opportunities to capitalize on your individual strengths.

Sometimes you'll be able to do this in a corporate setting. For example, in a company full of high Advantage (out for personal rewards) and high Activity (always busy) people, it can be a freeing and healing feeling to discover that you have more altruistic concerns. While everyone else is running around like crazed lemmings trying to solve a problem the boss needs answered today, your approach might be to shut your door, put your feet up on your desk with your hands clasped behind your head and your eyes shut, and come up with the ideal solution all by yourself. You can type up the answer in a memo, casually stroll down the hall to the boss's office while whistling a happy tune, and watch as the lemming-people pause just long enough to stare in disbelief.

At other times you may not have the flexibility to practice your uniqueness at work, though I believe smart managers will provide enough freedom for employees to implement their own personal styles. But I am well aware that many companies insist on strict conformity.

If you aren't able to practice your uniqueness at work, be sure to do it elsewhere. Be yourself at home. If you've been trying to follow all the "authoritative" books or advice of your parents in raising your kids, maybe it's time you found your own style. If you're an outdoor person who works sixty hours every week in a windowless cubicle, plan some weekend getaways with the family. Do whatever it takes to nurture the person you are deep down inside.

If you come to the conclusion that you're not suited for the type of work you're in, or for the particular work environment in which you spend most of your waking hours, you might want to look into career counseling. It may be intimidating or even frightening to consider making a major change, but if you're changing to something that will utilize your innate strengths, you won't regret making the effort to overcome your inertia.

Step #4: Find a "jigsaw puzzle" where you fit.

Finally, to make the healing of old emotional wounds complete, try to find a place where you are really, truly needed. Good teams are like jigsaw puzzles where one person picks up right where someone else leaves off. And if you find all the right pieces and get them in the proper order, the individual pieces become parts of a whole. The effects of synergy then take over, and the whole is greater than the sum of the separate parts.

In addition, nothing is more therapeutic for those old wounds than finding a perfect match of your talents (and interests) to an existing need. (See chapters 8 and 13 dealing with the importance of finding a place to fit in.)

At this point it's enough for you to be assured that your skills can be put to good use. You may be surprised to find yourself being drawn from a Fortune 500 conglomerate to a small struggling company. You may discover that you'd rather be in a service organization than a for-profit industry. Or you may not change jobs, yet will become much more effective as you put into practice your evolving skills.

In time and with proper care and concern, all but the most serious emotional wounds will heal without calling in a professional. You may have a few emotional scars for a while, but like most of your physical scars, they will soon be forgotten. And when you do happen to notice one from time to time, it will only serve to remind you of how far you've come. You might even be able to point to it someday and say to a younger colleague, "You know, that reminds me of a story you might find interesting. . . ."

CHAPTER 8

NEW PERCEPTIONS, IMPROVED RELATIONSHIPS

Suppose foreign agents were to kidnap you and smuggle you back to their homeland. Only too late do they discover they have the wrong person. (They meant to nab that strange neighbor of yours, but wrote down the wrong address.) Then, rather than risk getting caught by returning you to your home, they simply abandon you in a remote section of their country.

You have no idea where in the world you are. You don't speak the language. You can't make out any of the words on the signs because the alphabet is apparently nothing like your own. You stick out like a sore thumb, and you can tell from the furtive glances of the natives that no one trusts you. They're as suspicious of you as you are of them.

You wander aimlessly for a while, not knowing what to do. Eventually you come upon a small town and discover what seems to be a bookstore. In the window are titles in the native language—whatever it is. But there amid all the books, you see one word you recognize: *English*. Rushing inside, you discover that this book is a dictionary to convert English into the local language, and vice versa. You carry the dictionary to the store owner. After much confusion and difficulty, you finally point to enough words to make him understand that you would like to find an embassy or even a single person who speaks

English. He picks up the phone, jabbers in his mystery language, pauses, and then hands the phone to you. A voice at the other end says, "Hello. May I help you?" And soon your troubles are over.

Various behaviors are something like various languages. There's nothing wrong with any of them, and people who "speak the same language" understand each other just fine. But foreign behaviors (those unlike our own) may prevent effective communication. Sometimes we try diligently to understand people who don't behave like us in any way. At other times we give up on attempting to figure people out. It's much easier to write them off as strange, weird, or uncaring.

The trouble is that we're always in the minority. Many more people have behaviors that *vary* from ours than behaviors that are similar to our own. Our communication with them is impaired because we aren't able to "translate" their behaviors into a language we can understand and relate to. I hope this book has begun to convince you that while people's behaviors may be quite diverse, they can be equally worthwhile. And I hope you are beginning to have a desire to see past your own style of behavior and attempt to interpret the behaviors of others.

It may be difficult to accurately translate the behaviors of other people at first, though it gets easier with practice. Once you discover some of the basics, you'll begin to piece together a more accurate understanding of what motivates others to do what they do. That's also why it's so important to try to understand and analyze your own personality. As you examine and begin to comprehend all the variables that combine to make *you* so unique, you can better see how those variables could form other combinations and personalities.

In the last chapter, we examined some distorted self-perceptions that frequently cause emotional wounds if left unchallenged. In this chapter, we want to shift from an internal look to an examination of our *external* behaviors. Just as we can heal old wounds by understanding ourselves better, we can also build or strengthen relationships with others when we give them the freedom to behave differently from ourselves.

You and Your Parents

Probably no personality differences are as apparent as those be-tween parent and child. We can date lots of people and find a spouse who is a good match. We learn through trial and error whom we prefer to have as close friends. But the parent/child relationship is determined for us. We don't get to choose our parents or our children.

The same closeness that bonds families together can also cause intense frustration and confusion when personalities differ and no freedom is allowed for individual expression. Think back to the argu-ments you had with your parents when you were a child. What kinds of things did you tend to fight about?

In many cases, sources of parent/child conflict can be traced to some very basic personality differences. The parent has his or her own set of interests, active behaviors, needs, and reactive behaviors. The child has another. Yet the parent often suggests to the child, "This is the way you should behave. Be more like me." And the child, responding to his or her own personality components, thinks, *No thanks. I want to be my own person. It's your job to understand me.*

To the extent that the parent is able and willing to provide leeway for the child, the communication problem can be resolved. Yet a busy or authoritarian parent often misunderstands the child's need for self-expression. It may be interpreted as disobedience, rebellion, apathy, disrespect, or some other negative characteristic. Conse-quently, the child may be punished or disciplined simply for trying to figure out who he or she really is. The child's compliance leads either to a reluctant conformity to parental behaviors or further outward defiance. Both can be harmful to the relationship.

The problem can be especially severe when basic personalities of parent and child are in diagonal quadrants of the Life Style Grid. For example, suppose the father is in the red quadrant—a hands-on kind of guy who is direct in communication and is task-oriented. He enjoys mechanical things, working with tools, and so forth. Then suppose he has a son who is in the blue quadrant. The boy is quiet and reflective and likes people a lot more than machinery. He would rather sit and read than get out with Dad to work on the car or build things. In such a case, the more the father tries to shape the boy into his (the father's) own image, the weaker their relationship is likely to become. Perhaps the boy will grow up to think of himself as a failure for not living up to Dad's expectations. Or at the other extreme, maybe he chooses to try to please Dad at any cost.

As children move through adolescence, it's extremely important for them to redefine their relationships with their parents. Sometimes adult children continue to defer their own interests, needs, and other components of personality to please their parents. It would be much better for them to first identify and establish their own natural personalities and then reestablish the relationship with the parent on an adult-to-adult level rather than child-to-adult.

In some cases problems may arise because the parent never learned to express his or her own personality. Some parents attempt to maintain the same expectations that were imposed upon them, passing them on to the next generation without even knowing why. Yet the demands may be so specific and ingrained that it becomes next to impossible to know where parental expectations leave off and individual personal beliefs begin.

We can love and respect our parents without becoming absolute clones of them. But if we're not given the freedom to establish our own identities as children, we must demand the right as adults. The parent/child relationship will not be healthy if either party is denying his or her own personal uniqueness.

You and Your Children

If you can recall and relate to a significant degree of difficulty in establishing your own personality, you may not need to be reminded to avoid making the same mistakes with your children. Yet we occasionally fall into patterns that make no sense.

Even when we're aware of all the variables and challenges of child-rearing, it may seem strange that loving our children *equally* doesn't necessarily mean treating them *alike*. If we realize that each of our children will have his or her own individual and unique personality, we should also see that they are likely to require individual and unique motivation and discipline as well. We should not expect a single system of punishment or reward to be equally effective with all the different personality types.

It doesn't take long for children to begin to send out signals about their unique personalities. Even before they are able to speak, we can observe many significant traits that reveal their interests and needs. If you have children, I challenge you to go back to the components of personality listed in chapter 6 and see what traits you can detect about each child. In what areas do they demonstrate similar behaviors? In what areas are they different?

In the weeks and months to come, continue to watch their actions and see if they confirm your initial instincts. As you learn to differentiate personality types, you may be surprised to see how well you begin to relate to your children as individuals. You will quickly begin to pick up various ways to reward them, motivate them, and discipline them.

For example, the promise of a trip to the park may excite two out of three of them. But the third may prefer to build a kite to fly in the park. Sending them to their rooms as punishment may work for some kids, but others would welcome the solitude! You need to be wise and discriminating in your choice of incentives.

As your children grow older, you can talk to them to learn what you need to know about their interests and attitudes. Not only will this communication give *you* insight into their actions, it will also help *them* think through their uniqueness. As they see that you care about them as individuals—not just as "Kid #2"—they will feel free to begin to establish their own identities. They can still be aware that you might hope they all become attorneys like Dad, but they also know you're giving them the license to pursue their own interests and goals.

It's never too early to begin to foster the development of individuality in your children. Nor is it ever too late. As you do so, you may have to reconsider the advice of some of the parenting materials available. Any resource that suggests a single method of child-rearing, promising results for every child, should be taken with a grain of salt. Keep looking until you find authors who recognize the unique characteristics of children. Then adapt their ideas to fit your child, rather than the other way around.

You and Your Spouse

For most people, a marriage bond will be the single most important relationship in their lives. The husband/wife relationship is the foundation for all others. If it is strong and growing, other relationships (with children, friends, and coworkers) are likely to flourish as well. If is it not as strong as it should be, it is likely that other relationships will suffer too.

Yet even within the marriage bond it is possible for misperceptions to occur. Though you know your spouse better than probably anyone else on earth, what you don't know can still weaken the relationship.

It has already been noted that we should be aware of "courtship behavior" during the early stages of a relationship when both you and the people you date are on best behavior. At these times, your actions don't necessarily reflect your genuine feelings or personality.

Of course, it's natural to want to present yourself in the best possible light to those who might play a major role in your future. (This is true of prospective employers as well as prospective husbands or wives.) The potential trouble lies in not being willing to drop the facade of being your best possible self to reveal your usual self. Some people seem to fear that such a metamorphosis would be far too frightening and threatening for the other person to take.

But if you never reveal who you really are during your dating or engagement period, it becomes even harder to do so after the wedding ceremony. One or both newlyweds might be repressing "normal" behaviors. Yet the confession of such behaviors is usually far less destructive than trying to keep them hidden. Indeed, the sooner the real person comes out, the sooner the couple can get to know each other at a more intimate level.

Yet some people insist on trying to keep certain aspects of their personalities hidden. She doesn't want him to find out that her mother cooked most of those wonderful meals she took credit for when they were dating. He doesn't want her to discover that as much as he loves watching PBS with her, he'd much rather spend an occasional Thursday night with his old bowling chums. Her unconfessed lottery fever continues, though secretly. His outdoor interests are now limited to puttering around the yard. And so it goes. Any single one of these incidents is so minor as to seem inconsequential. But in time, dozens of little things begin to add up and, before you know it, both husband and wife are ready to explode at each other without actually knowing why.

Young couples need to learn to be open and honest with each other. Only when they begin to understand where each other stands in regard to the individual components of personality will they be able to plan their life together effectively. They may be giving up things unnecessarily. They may discover a lot of mutual interests that neither has yet expressed. They may be able to schedule times to be alone or to pursue interests the other doesn't share and still have plenty of time to build their relationship together.

As we have said previously, the truth seldom hurts as much as trying to avoid the truth. Many of our problems can be resolved only after we take a long, clear look at ourselves and the personalities of the people we care about.

Plan to spend a couple of hours with your spouse for the sole purpose of evaluating your personalities. Be honest. Take a look at the individual components of personality, including interests (Artistic, Clerical, Literary, Mechanical, Musical, Numerical, Outdoor, Persuasive, Scientific, and Social Services) and active behavior/needs. Interview each other as to perceived strengths and weaknesses. Then, after each self-assessment, let the other person comment. See if your perceptions agree. When you find areas you disagree on or aren't sure of, let those be your "homework assignments." When a relevant situation comes up during the next week or month, see how you respond to it. Or, if appropriate, look for a neutral third party to provide additional observations and insight.

Informal, regular discussions can go a long way toward bringing couples closer together. In fact, my company has devised a helpful evaluation for couples (or other people who plan to spend a lot of time together) called "Differences to Watch." We identify the components in which the couple is farthest apart and then provide advice for how each person should treat the other when stressful situations arise because of these differences.

We have received tremendous response to this service. For example, one wife says:

> After being married for seventeen years, my husband and I didn't think a computer-generated form was going to tell us anything we didn't already know about ourselves. But we were quite surprised. Two components that were red-flagged for us were Change and Freedom. In each case, his Needs score was considerably higher than mine. We knew this assessment was accurate because we have recurring discussions about his wanting to move, change jobs, and do other things that I perceive as too risky. I am much more resistant to change.
>
> But the biggest difference was in the Empathy area. Our Needs scores were pretty close, but the Active Behavior was drastically different. (He was a 3 on the scale and I was 85.) I've always wanted him to show more emotion, and he seems to perceive my "touchy feely" tendencies as a weakness. The reports that accompanied the scores helped us understand that neither of us was necessarily right or wrong. It showed us how we could relate to each other while respecting the differences in our basic personalities. Consequently, we now feel much more freedom to be ourselves. I know my husband expresses love in the way that is most natural for him, even though it may not be exactly what I'm looking for at the moment. And he knows there are times when he needs to go beyond his "normal" expressions of empathy and show more emotion than is natural for him.
>
> As it turned out, that questionnaire led to a significant improvement in our marriage.

People who spend a lot of time together shouldn't require a computer-generated form to alert them to recurring problem areas. They can go a long way in determining their own "differences to watch." And once such things are identified and brought out into the open, the solutions are usually quite apparent. As soon as two people are honest enough to express themselves—"When we get angry at each other, you always rant and rave while I withdraw into my shell. How do you think we should handle this in the future?"—then they can determine a workable solution.

Yet sometimes a third party is needed to bring fresh insight to a couple who may be too close to each other to see the problem. One of our consultants was once put in the position of impromptu marriage counselor. A couple she knew who had always wanted to visit Paris finally got their wish. When the couple returned, the consultant saw the husband and innocently asked, "So, how was your trip?" He shot back, "Our marriage is falling apart, and we've charged it all to American Express!"

The consultant knew the couple well enough to know that the husband had the personality profile of a consummate romantic. The wife was much more logical. But they had been in complete agreement that going to Paris would be the trip of a lifetime. Naturally, they were confused as to why the trip had caused problems rather than bringing them closer together.

After his wife joined him, the consultant asked the husband, "What was your expectation of an ideal day in Paris?" He replied, "I thought we would wake up and make a little love. Then we'd have a continental breakfast, do a little sightseeing, go back to the room, and make some more love before lunch. Then we'd take a nap in preparation for going out on the town at night. After some dancing and a late dinner, we'd go back to the room and make love." (It doesn't take a trained psychologist to see a pattern here!) The consultant turned to the wife, who is a professional dress designer, and asked, "What was *your* expectation of an ideal day in Paris?" She replied, "Ever since I was in school, I've dreamed of going either to Rome or Paris, the fashion capitals of the world. There's just so much to see in Paris. I wanted to spend at least three days in the Louvre. I wanted to visit all the houses of fashion. I wanted to go to the West Bank and spend some time in the artistic community." Then the woman turned to her husband and said, "Honey, I love you, but we can make love at home."

This couple worked everything out. But theirs is a classic example of how two people can apparently agree, yet have extremely diverse underlying needs. They both had dreamed for years of going to Paris, but had never actually discussed *why*. When they got there and discovered that neither was aware of the needs of the other, significant problems resulted.

The process of examining the components of personality can be helpful to any married couple. Almost every couple will be able to determine one or more recurring areas of conflict. With a little discussion and deduction, the problem areas can likely be traced back to one of the components. The couple can then focus on active behavior, needs, and reactive behavior in order to come to a better understanding of each other. The next time the same problem arises, they know they have done some groundwork upon which they can continue to search for more lasting solutions.

You and Your Friends

By now you should be getting the idea of what to look for in relationships. But the difference is that in most of the previous examples, there is a built-in incentive to do something about it. We have no choice but to deal with parents, spouse, and children. Friendships, on the other hand, are something we choose to develop and they must be nurtured.

Most of us find ourselves drawn to certain individuals. In most cases we are attracted to people we understand—those who are most similar to ourselves in terms of basic personality. In other cases I would agree that "opposites attract." A quiet girl may be close friends with a real "people person." She can stay in the shadows, so to speak, but still have a fairly active social life because of her outgoing friend.

Yet most of us have opportunities for close friendships that are never realized because we're too quick to give up on certain people. If there are few similarities or no apparent natural attraction between us, we may simply "write them off." But if you truly believe the principles set forth in this book, it may be time for you to increase your levels of acceptance.

Do you really believe that everyone has unique strengths and contributions to make? Do you believe that all basic personalities are good—even those that may be nothing like your own? Do you believe that your way of doing things, while fine for you, may not necessarily be best for everyone?

If you *really* believe all these things, you may be beginning to recognize the potential in some of the people you have not previously been drawn to. I would predict that there are people in your neighborhood, workplace, church, health club, and other arenas that you have avoided because you didn't think you would "click." If so, I challenge you to give them another chance.

Try talking to some of these people again. Question them about their interests. Attempt to determine their needs. Watch their active and reactive behaviors. Try to figure out what quadrant of the Life Style Grid these people belong in. Challenge yourself to work as hard at getting to know them as you've worked to avoid them in the past.

You may not become best friends with any of these people, but the experience will be good for you. We all need to do more than just *know* that people are different. We need to truly gain insight into various kinds of personalities and come to respect the basic differences between us.

The fact of the matter is that we *need* people who are different from ourselves. A group of Blue people can hang around together and spend hour upon hour in introspection and long-range planning . . . and never get around to actually *doing* anything. The Red people can be blunt and aggressive with each other and get along just fine, but they will do much better to make friends among the Yellows and Blues, who can give them some creative ideas and plans to put in place the systems to direct Reds' activities.

All of us need support systems (or networks) to function most effectively. Though we can teach ourselves to do the things that need doing, it's never as good as having the help and advice of others who genuinely enjoy and excel at the tasks we dread. I will say more about this in the chapter on team building (chapter 13). But for now you can begin to do some initial work on your own to expand your circle of associates.

At first, you may feel as if you're in a land where you don't speak the language and no one speaks yours. But it's surprising to see how quickly you'll learn to translate. Remember that you're entering the relationship with the knowledge that people are all wonderfully different, and you should have a certain level of acceptance by now. Other people won't necessarily have the same body of working knowledge. They may tend to be more uncomfortable with and even suspicious of you. You may need to be patient and persevering at first. But the friendships that come from your selfless actions will be well worth the effort.

Why Bother?

The importance of building stronger relationships may be more apparent to some people than others. If you have a high Empathy score, you are going to place more importance on the feelings that occur in your interactions with other people. But others might ask: "What's the big deal? Isn't it enough for me to simply be myself and let other people worry about themselves? Why should I impose myself on them?"

There may be several reasons why we are reluctant to form new friendships. For one thing, we simply may not know how. We may have been waiting for the other person to take the initiative. Some may have been "burned" in the past and are not eager to get involved in new relationships. Others may have been taught as children to keep to themselves and shut out the rest of the world. Yet despite the various reasons for our initial reticence, people need other people.

And the very fact that so many diverse personalities exist would seem to indicate that we should draw upon one another's strengths.

Besides, wouldn't you like to be known as the kind of person who brings out the best in others? In a work setting, that's a valuable skill. In a social environment, it's an enviable ability.

There are already too many barriers that prevent people from working (and playing) together. It's a shame when mere differences in personality keep people apart rather than motivating them to depend on each other instead. Perhaps your new understanding of personality components will allow you to be a facilitator in combatting this problem.

A Few Questions

Ask yourself the following questions. Some you will be able to answer with no trouble. Others are likely to take longer. Don't rush through them. Take your time and try to determine the best possible answers for each one.

1. Name four relatively close friends who represent each quadrant of the Birkman Life Style Grid. If you cannot, what area(s) is missing? Why do you think some areas have few, if any, names that immediately come to mind?
2. Think of any recent personality conflicts you may have had. If you had been aware of the various components of personality prior to the encounters, do you think some of the conflicts might have been avoided? What are some things you can do the next time a similar conflict arises?
3. What ongoing relationship is the weakest right now? (Spouse? Children? Parents? A close friend?) Based on what you've read so far, try to come up with a strategy for strengthening the relationship.
4. When you first meet a person, would you say you tend to focus more on your similarities or your differences? Why?

5. In what ways did your relationship with your parents change as you grew up and moved from a subservient relationship with them to more of a peer relationship? Was the change easy or difficult for you? Do you detect any unresolved tension that needs to be addressed now that you're an adult?

6. If you have children, to what extent have you been attempting to treat them uniquely rather than treating them equally? Based on the personality of each individual child, what would be an appropriate method of reward, punishment, and motivation?

7. Do you tend to shy away from people you don't understand? If so, why do you think that is true?

These questions should just get you started. Indeed, it will take a lifetime to build and strengthen your relationships. But before you go too far, read the next chapter. Just as you dealt with personal perceptions in the last chapter and interpersonal perceptions in this chapter, the next will provide you with an on-the-job approach to dealing with work perceptions and personalities.

CHAPTER 9

PERCEPTION AT WORK

When Lewis Carroll wrote of Alice's adventures through the looking glass, he was trying to create one of the most fanciful places imaginable. Things happened there that made absolutely no sense at all. The characters were eccentric, even bizarre. It was difficult for Alice to make friends, and she hardly ever knew what was going on. All she could do was wander around, interacting with all those weird creatures, and hope she could eventually get back to where she had come from.

But times have changed. I would venture to suggest that Alice had it easy compared to what many of us experience during an average day at work. Think about it. Don't you know a "white rabbit" who is perpetually rushing around from place to place, yet is almost always late to his very important dates?

How about Tweedledee and Tweedledum, the indistinguishable clones who adapt to the corporate culture so completely that they lose all traces of personal individuality?

Does your office have a Queen of Hearts, whose wrath is expressed when some whim goes unfulfilled? Her cry may not be "Off with his head!", but she is likely to have some equivalent threat intended to strike terror in the souls of her underlings.

Or maybe you know a Cheshire Cat, in whom one particular obnoxious characteristic stands out. Your version of this individual may not be known for an eerie smile as much as for a propensity to gossip, tell dirty jokes, run the office pools, or some other deviant behavior.

And of course you have your share of Mad Hatters, pushed-around doormouse types, mysterious caterpillars, and on and on. The characters you must deal with on a daily basis may make Alice's experience look like she was at a . . . well . . . at a tea party!

Just Another Set of Relationships

Maybe your own work setting isn't nearly as strange as the one described. Maybe you love your job, can't wait to get to work each morning, and can barely tear yourself away at night. But believe it or not, some people feel a great amount of stress and confusion in the workplace. They are pressured to perform to unrealistic expectations, and they sometimes have to work with people who don't seem to have a clue as to what's going on.

Yet whether your job is a joy or a joke, you can make it a better experience. After all, your job is just another set of relationships. Just as you can use the principles in this book to become a better parent, spouse, or individual, you can also adapt them to improving yourself as an employee or boss.

Even if your devotion to your job and fellow employees isn't nearly as strong as it is toward others in your life, the amount of *time* you spend at work is significant enough for you to try to make it a more productive experience. Many people spend more hours with fellow employees than with anyone else. So even though work relationships may not be a *top* priority, they should become a priority nevertheless.

Much of the work my company does is in regard to people in the workplace. We hear all kinds of stories from the employees and business leaders who come to us—horror stories, war stories, and some stories that sound more like fiction than fact. But regardless of the tale we are told, we try to help the person or the company construct their own happy ending.

Work should be enjoyable as well as productive. I have been fortunate enough to devote my entire life to a vocation that I would have chosen as a hobby if I couldn't make a living doing it. I try to help other people match themselves to their jobs. And once someone knows his or her interests, active behavior, needs, and reactive behavior, it becomes considerably easier to plug him or her into an appropriate job to fit that personality.

But since perfect matches aren't always possible, this chapter will be devoted to helping you do as well as you can *in the job you have now*. If you are terribly frustrated, try these suggestions. They have helped a lot of people work through severe problems and conflicts. But if you try them and still see no improvement, and if you seem to have no hope where you are, you might want to consider professional counseling to locate a different job where you can find fulfillment and productivity.

Managing Your Boss

Let's begin with your relationship with your boss. This is a major consideration in determining whether or not you enjoy your work. If you and your boss are best friends, you probably don't have many complaints about your job. But if you never quite know where you stand, or if you know you aren't pleasing your boss, then no amount of compensation is likely to make your work environment pleasant. This is a key relationship—one that demands regular attention and monitoring.

Start with his or her interests.

If you're like most people, you've probably already taken note of your boss's *interests*. (The sixteen golf trophies in the case behind her desk are a subtle hint regarding one of them.) And you've probably also scoped out the photos and art work in her office for other information. But then, so has everybody else. You're all looking at the same set of clues. A good detective, however, will piece together patterns based on those clues. For example, the golf trophies, a photo of a family camping trip, and a subscription to *Field and Stream* not only reveal specific interests but a general *outdoor* pattern. So, if you want to set a proper mood for a proposal during lunchtime, you might consider take-out food at a picnic table in the park rather than in a smoke-filled restaurant.

Or if you've observed a collection of gadgets in your boss's office, know that he frequently notices when equipment isn't working properly and goes to car shows every chance he gets, he's showing signs of a *mechanical* pattern. Perhaps inviting him to get more involved in your work at a hands-on level would be appreciated. You can make similar observations regarding music, numbers, artistic interests, and so forth. Be aware that a deeply rooted interest is probably going to permeate a person's entire way of thinking. You can use examples or object lessons based on these interests to get your points across more clearly. You can put him or her at ease (and be more at ease yourself) when the two of you are together for any length of time. As you reveal more about yourself in terms of related interests, you'll have his full attention rather than simply maintaining polite chitchat.

Identify his or her "color."

In addition, you need to try to determine your boss's "color" on our Life Style Grid. What characterizes his or her *active behavior*— the style of operation when he is at his best or when she is feeling good about herself? Observe your boss during stressless times, if possible. Then consult the chart on page 44 [chapter 4] to determine which of the quadrants best fits him or her.

The ability to "read" active behavior will be a big help. You can tell from subtle signs whether the boss is feeling pretty good or is under stress. But at this point a lot of people make mistakes based on erroneous assumptions. They think, *Hmmmm. The boss is at his best when he's being logical rather than emotional. He always seems to want us to make immediate decisions when presented with options.* So they never try to deal with him at a feelings level.

Don't make the same mistake. Remember Myth #3 from chapter 3: "The way a person acts is the way he or she needs to be treated." Not necessarily true. A person's Need score in any given component may be at the other end of the scale from his Active Behavior score. In some cases a boss who treats others in a logical and detached way may need to be treated in much the same way. But then again, he may personally *need* a lot of emotional support, even though he doesn't show emotion toward others. She might expect others to make decisions without a lot of thought, but *she* might want to weigh all the options and get advice from others before making a major decision.

Differentiate active behavior from needs.

Smart employees will look beyond the interests and the active behavior of the boss and will try to identify his or her needs. Of course, needs are usually well concealed, so this won't be easy. Watch as others relate to the boss. See what works and what doesn't. Then, through trial and error, you will be able to discover the areas where his active behavior differs from his needs. When you know why some things work and others don't, you can avoid many of the same mistakes that others make in their relationships with him.

A good boss will try to establish a feel for the individual strengths of the people who report to him or her, will be aware of the differences in personalities, and will try to ensure that everyone is involved personally rather than simply trying to accommodate to a single standard of expectation.

But let's assume that you don't have a good boss. What can you do to break out of the pack mentality of the person who holds your future in his or her hand?

Initiate change "from below" if you are able.

Try volunteering for the things you enjoy doing and that you know you do well. If it seems that your boss is simply trying to divvy up the workload into equal portions, you may as well work on the tasks that you know you can do better than anyone else. Make suggestions as to who would be good for other work that needs to be done. ("You know, Jack is a whiz when it comes to numbers crunching"; "Frieda is the best person I know with promotional ideas.") If your boss isn't willing to do any team building, maybe *you* can initiate it.

Most bosses will be satisfied if their employees make them look good in the eyes of the higher-ups in the company. And if you can devise a plan that will increase the productivity of your division, your boss should be willing to give it a try. In the meantime, perhaps you can at least carve out a little niche where you will feel better about what *you* do.

When You're the Boss

Then again, maybe *you're* the boss or have some degree of influence in the corporate structure. When people report to you, take advantage of the situation and begin to practice what you've been learning about perception and personality.

Your color or combination of colors describes your unique style of managing—your unique goals, your approach, what motivates you to lead, what happens to you under stress, and the kind of environment you prefer. By knowing your colors, you will be able to compare your managing style with those you manage.

Knowing your *true colors* will help you manage a diversity of people and maximize their effectiveness individually and in group settings. As you gain more knowledge of the strengths of your style, you can increase your managerial effectiveness by recognizing the areas of probable conflict between those for whom you are responsible. The colors give you a preliminary understanding of the differences between usual behavior and motivational needs. This will enable you to pinpoint likely areas of interpersonal stress and the appropriate action for managing stress.

Are You the Green Manager?

Relationships with Peers and Employees

Green managers try to be friendly and cordial and motivate others by persuasion and encouragement. While appearing to be friendly, however, they also have an air of casual detachment and aloofness. If given an opportunity, they prefer to give general instructions on a personal and individual basis. They get the greatest sense of satisfaction from talking and exchanging ideas with other people.

Approaches to Relationships and Management Team Building

Green managers initially tend to select verbal and friendly individuals who prefer conversation over detailed work or long-range planning activities. Mature Green managers, however, will realize the need for delegating authority and selecting individuals who can attend to routine and detailed assignments.

Communication

The communication range of Green managers can extend from friendly and lengthy to argumentative and excessive. During times of stress or pressure, they prefer a strategy involving rationalization and excuses. In addition, conversations can either become confrontational and argumentative or evasive and superficial. During stressful times, it is difficult to keep the Green manager's conversations consistently objective and "on-task."

Decision-Making and Problem-Solving

Green managers tend to make snap judgments or impulsive decisions. High, restless energy coupled with short attention span results in a preference for quick and simple resolutions.

Creativity and Planning

Green managers enjoy the world of ideas. Their emphasis is on promotion of subtle persuasion, and they expect similar types of verbally competitive approaches from others.

Organizing and Controlling

Green managers require a great deal of personal freedom within the job structure and willingly grant similar freedom to others. They expect everyone to be self-starting and self-motivating. They prefer the use of persuasion; argument and verbal skills give them the appearance of "hit-and-run" managers when under pressure (i.e., a brief verbal encounter followed by little, if any, follow-through).

Business Procedures

They have minimal use for formal business procedures. An inexperienced Green manager will neglect routine policy and procedure, while a more seasoned manager will have learned to delegate detail. At times, they appear to have invented and defined the word *unconventional*.

The Green Manager's Main Motivational Needs:

1. friendly and casual relationships with peers
2. stimulating and changing work environment
3. promotional and competitive setting

Areas for Personal Growth and Organizational Development:

1. understanding of own interpersonal needs
2. acceptance of human differences, both behavioral and motivational
3. effective control of excessive nervous energy (i.e., exercise, relaxation, etc.)
4. attention span and time-management program

Are You the Blue Manager?

Relationships with Peers and Employees

More than anything else, Blue managers want to be valued. They tend to seek job opportunities that provide a "home away from home." They feel people are best motivated by kindness and friendship and do not enjoy the title or duties of "boss." Blue managers believe that direct orders disturb or offend others so they prefer to suggest or ask. They are convinced that if you treat others nicely, those persons will respond in similar ways. Managing is thought of as a way of expressing goodwill to others. Money and status are not valued for any intrinsic worth but rather as tools to ensure admiration and friendship. They treat subordinates as equals or friends and tend to be overly trusting and dependent upon work-based relationships.

Approaches to Relationships and Management Team Building

Blue managers tend to select subordinates who meet a respect and friendship need, since the Blue manager is attracted to cooperative and low-key individuals.

Communication

Communication is seldom factual or to-the-point. Those communicating with Blue managers either (1) get a minimal response, or (2) leave with the feeling that nothing was decided or resolved. Blue managers try to generate a friendly and comfortable (if inconclusive) environment. Discussions are usually kept on a personal level.

Decision-Making and Problem-Solving

Blue managers tend to delay decisions until almost ineffective. They base their decisions more on the well-being of individuals concerned than on productivity.

Creativity and Planning

They enjoy the world of concepts, ideas, and plans. Major problem areas for Blue managers are (1) confining planning to realistic considerations, and (2) initiating the necessary action to implement plans.

Competition

Blue managers view the world from a "live-and-let-live" perspective and prefer to aid others or give favors rather than compete or invite confrontation.

Organizing and Controlling

Blue managers are very tolerant and permissive; they do not like to order people around or organize their activities for them and would rather not correct others or evaluate their activities. In terms of controlling, they don't care to know all the petty office activities and gossip. They prefer not to have to give strong direction based on office data. They function best when responsibilities do not require close control of personnel or systems.

Business Procedures

Blue managers have little use for formal business procedures, and rationalize that formality only tends to negate affiliation and good feelings. To them, policy is less important than personal considerations in the attempt to please coworkers and employees (e.g., "We'll make an exception in this case").

The Blue Manager's Main Motivational Needs:

1. affiliation with significant others and esteem from peers
2. support and validation from friends
3. pleasant and cooperative work associations

Areas for Personal Growth and Organizational Development:

1. admittance of interpersonal needs
2. acceptance of human differences, both behavioral and motivational
3. positive self-assertion and constructive use of disagreement
4. acceptance of the fact that the best interests of everyone are served by meeting the needs of the organization

Are You the Red Manager?

Relationships with Peers and Employees

Red managers are objective and dominant. They have difficulty delegating authority. Ideas and instructions are often expressed as impersonal and objective orders or, when under pressure, as commands. They view others either as easily dominated or as competitors and are often unaware of or refuse to recognize the negative impact their behavior has on others. Red managers readily criticize poor performance, give no feedback for average performance, and rarely praise good performance.

Approaches to Relationships and Management Team Building

Subordinates are often hired because Red managers perceive that they can be dominated. Forceful and dominant supervisors meet Reds' need to compete. Less dominant supervisors are viewed as weak or vulnerable to manipulation.

Communication

Discussions and meetings with Red managers appear to suffer from one-way communication. These managers often give the appearance of having little desire to listen and may appear to try to "score points" rather than reach a satisfactory compromise or mutual agreement in conferences. They tend to become argumentative or to lecture rather than to encourage reciprocity, and are prone to ask penetrating and unexpected questions that put others at a disadvantage.

Decision-Making and Problem-Solving

Red managers tend to be highly autocratic. Important decisions are often made independently of peer or employee input and subsequently passed down as mandates. Decisions may be hasty, impulsive, subject to change, and are often made without adequate preparation or data.

Creativity and Planning

Red managers prefer not to plan or invest time in "ideas." They view job performance as a function of "doing," not "thinking." Occasionally, new or good ideas are received and passed on as if they were one's own. These managers feel extremely pressured when asked to plan, project future requirements, or produce a creative approach, yet because of a strong need to dominate, they often have difficulty delegating these tasks.

Competition

In conflict situations, Red managers view people interaction from an "I win, you lose" perspective. They view their own performance in a similar manner—consistently setting higher goals for self-accomplishment.

Organizing and Controlling

Red managers prefer not to systematize in any great detail, and encounter problems when required to account carefully for activities or to document work and accomplishments. If in a managerial position, objectives are set (if not well-defined), and subordinates are required to implement. If in an employee situation, they may react strongly to new procedures and objectives that require additional time and detail.

The Red Manager's Main Motivational Needs:

1. power, authority, and dominance
2. independence and freedom from accountability
3. tangible rewards for personal accomplishment

Areas for Personal Growth and Organizational Effectiveness:

1. better understanding of own interpersonal needs
2. acceptance of human differences, both behavioral and motivational
3. improvement of listening skills
4. more appreciation for the impact of feelings both in self and in others
5. acceptance of the need to adhere to organization requirements and policies

Are You the Yellow Manager?

Relationships with Peers and Employees

Yellow managers tend to be impersonal and casual, with communication guarded and words carefully weighed. A reluctance to engage in discussion or conversation is further emphasized by a restrained manner. These managers tend to be detached and aloof when relaying methods, procedures, and tasks from superiors to subordinates. Yellow managers base performance appraisal of subordinates on the ability to (1) follow rules and (2) keep a low profile. They assume that people "are what they are" and cannot be motivated and developed. They are reluctant to accept new responsibility and more reluctant to delegate.

Approaches to Relationships and Management Team Building

The concept of team building or group cooperation is difficult to accept. The most comfortable position for Yellow managers is one of (1) letting someone else select the team, (2) staying removed from active participation in group discussion, and (3) monitoring, evaluating, and often discounting team efforts. When given an opportunity to hire employees, they may select those with a tendency to work carefully, require minimum supervision and verbal instructions, and "keep a low profile."

Communication

Meetings and discussions seem to suffer from no-way communication! Verbal interaction is minimal and there is a strong reluctance to share information. When asked a specific question, Yellow managers may respond with a specific and limited answer. Otherwise, communication is guarded, infrequent, and completely shuts down when discussions are perceived as threatening.

Decision-Making and Problem-Solving

Yellow managers hesitate to face major decisions or to solve major problems. They would much prefer to accumulate information in the problem-solving process and leave final decisions to superiors.

Creativity and Planning

Yellow managers are reluctant to try new approaches or to initiate new plans, and tend to stick to past or present policy. When organizational breakdowns suggest a need for new approaches, a reluctance to change becomes evident. These managers focus on a safer approach requiring tighter control and more attention to existing procedure.

Competition

Yellow managers have a basic dislike for competitive situations. Their usual response to conflict and competition is to withdraw, document, or prepare a "Pearl Harbor File" for defense.

Organizing and Controlling

Controlling is a favored function because it is a way to ensure stability and to monitor the amount of change going on in an organization. If change or slippage is detected, the reasons generally are not sought. Instead, monitors and tighter controls are used. Organizing is not a desired or welcome function of the Yellow manager. They do not view organizing as a function for growth but rather as a means for stabilizing relationships, defining responsibilities, and slowing down change.

Business Procedures

Yellow managers are sticklers for organizational policy, procedure, and guidelines. They derive a strong sense of security by following policy "to the letter." In times of upheaval, they believe in following the book.

The Yellow Manager's Main Motivational Needs:

1. security and stability
2. predictable life situations and low-profile employees
3. minimal personal contact

Areas for Personal Growth and Organizational Development:

1. understanding of own interpersonal needs
2. acceptance of human differences, both behavioral and motivational
3. tolerance of others' social needs
4. exposure to and acceptance of change

Put an end to senseless tradition.

Begin by questioning all the assumptions that are being made. Most companies have routine methods of operating and long-standing traditions, yet aren't able to explain why they do things in a certain way. Patterns were established, probably for some good reason, but so long ago that they may no longer be feasible. One result of such traditions is that people may be performing unnecessary tasks. Perhaps reports are regularly being written, typed, corrected, photocopied, sent out, and filed. But how many people want, need, or even read the reports? The perception may be that a lot of work is getting done when the reality is that many people are involved in needless activities.

Your employees probably have plenty of work that actually *needs* doing. Don't look at the situation through the same set of lenses as your predecessor. Take a clear and objective look. Dare to have a fresh set of perceptions to work by and act on what you determine to be true.

Build mini-teams.

Consider slight (but significant) shifts in the work responsibilities of the people who report to you. As you perceive which of your team members belongs in each of the quadrants, you may be able to assign them more comfortable and productive responsibilities. If one person is miserable working with numbers while another person loves numeric tasks, you could "stack the deck" of assignments rather than dealing out equal amounts of numbers work to each person. In exchange, the person who hates numbers will be able to do a lot more of what he or she is really good at, and can help out the other person in one of his weak areas.

As much as possible, build mini-teams. I would hope team building is being done on a corporate scale. There is much profit and power in recognizing individual strengths and putting teams together that cover all the bases, yet allow each person to maximize the things he or she does well. But even if this is not the corporate approach to getting work done, perhaps it can be *your* approach in the area you oversee. When individuals are focusing most of their time on the things they do best, not only will productivity go up, so will morale. (Chapter 13 will have more to say about team building.)

Keep everyone operating in their active behaviors.

Finally, as you grow more proficient in reading the behaviors and personalities of the people you oversee, you'll learn how to differentiate between their active behaviors (the things they do when they are feeling good about themselves) and their reactive behaviors (how they act under stress). Your goal should be to keep everyone in "active mode."

It doesn't matter how good a team you assemble if they aren't then allowed to work according to their natural styles. When they feel so much stress that they begin to kick into reactive behaviors, it's like a chain reaction. One person feels pressured or fatigued and reacts defensively to a situation rather than taking positive action. In response, someone else then becomes reactive and, before you know it, you have a whole "team" of nonproductive people. Some will be too aggressive, some will withdraw and shut down, and others will spin their wheels without accomplishing anything.

To offset this possibility, monitor the stress level at regular intervals. A good team will pull together when the pressure is on unless the weight of the assignment or deadline is entirely too heavy or unrealistic. Regulating stress is much easier than regrouping after the team has exploded into reactive behavior.

Strengthening Peer Relationships

Everyone is aware of the importance of the boss/employee relationship, but we may overlook the potential that lies in getting to know our colleagues better. Again, we tend to be drawn to people who are much like ourselves—same interests, same operating style. This is true at work as well as anywhere else.

Build bridges to other "colors."

There is a wealth of potential in those who differ from us and it will pay to expand your circle of associates at work. Failing to understand what motivates those people, you may have tended to leave them alone. But with a little effort, you'll discover that some of them can become your best allies.

For example, I recall a situation in which my company was called in for outplacement counseling. The comptroller of a company was about to be fired. His boss had foreseen no problems during the interview and first few months of work. But suddenly the person just wasn't getting the job done. We found that the comptroller had a high need for structure and wasn't getting enough direction from his boss. Consequently, he would freeze rather than take responsibility for a task and run with it. We suggested that the boss be more direct with this employee. He agreed to try, and the comptroller's work improved significantly. Rather than letting the person go, the working relationship became so satisfactory that the two eventually became close friends.

Be on the lookout for reactive behaviors.

Due to the constant stress of a pressure-filled environment, it may be rare to see people operating at their best. Don't be tempted to judge their performance or attitude based on your perceptions of them under these conditions.

In "reactive mode," someone may say or do something that is not at all typical of the person's normal behavior. Yet if we take the comment personally, we may immediately kick into our own reactive behavior. Some of us would retaliate with an even more scathing comment. Some of us would cry. Some of us would withdraw into our shells. But none of these behaviors would address the problem.

At my company, we have discovered a secret for dealing with the reactive behaviors of other people. If you know what their normal, active behaviors are, you can adopt that behavior in putting out the fire. For example, if the person is usually a touching (tactile) individual who puts a lot of emotion into communications, you can approach him or her with a reassuring hand on the shoulder or a gentle inquiry. Such an approach may not be your own natural, active behavior. Yet by adapting to the other person's style of effective communication, you relieve some of the stress and make possible a resolution to the problem.

Know your limitations.

Obviously, you can't spend all your time acting in the best interests of other people and ignoring your own needs. If you're a Yellow person who is trying to build bridges to Reds, Greens, and Blues by ignoring their reactive behaviors and modeling your behavior to meet their needs, you'll quickly become frustrated or lose track of yourself.

Even a sensitive boss or coworker won't always be able to read your needs, so carve out some time for yourself. If you've been sacrificing an outdoor interest and a high freedom need in order to spend time with other people indoors, you might want to plan a picnic lunch for a couple of days until you're "stoked up" again. If you have a high empathy need but have been relating to other people who like to keep things emotionless, plan time with someone who can give you some emotional "hugs."

Don't stretch yourself so thin that you become just as reactive as everyone else. Be sure to maintain your own emotional well-being as you tend to others.

What Happened to Perception?

Having branched out into a study of interests, needs, active behaviors, reactive behaviors, and personality in general, you may be wondering what all this has to do with the topic of perception. But I hope you see how important it is to maintain accurate perceptions in all of these areas. If you make observations without bothering to differentiate between natural, active behavior and stress-induced, reactive behavior, your perceptions are likely to mislead you.

What I hope you are learning to do is to *manage* your perceptions. Your eyes won't often deceive you, but your brain will. The things you witness are usually correct, but the conclusions you reach based on those observations can be quite erroneous.

Wrong perceptions can cause deep and lasting emotional wounds in regard to self-image. They can damage our closest relationships—with spouse, parents, children, and friends. And they can make the workplace a dreaded environment. But as we learn to manage those perceptions—to see past our initial assumptions to discover a deeper level of truth—the key areas of our lives take on a new and more healing perspective.

You may be in a job (or other position) trying hard to perceive yourself as being on top of things and in the right place, yet never actually feeling right about it. If so, deal with the feelings. Manage your perceptions. Don't let the confusion continue when you might be able to make some positive changes.

Some time ago we were called by the internal consultant of a large company to consult with a seven-person division of that company. It didn't take long, however, to determine that the internal consultant was in the wrong job. She was not very good at team building and most other "people" functions. By her own admission, she was much better at systems, writing manuals, and other reflective activities. In fact, the closer we looked, the more obvious it became that *most* of the people in this division were in the wrong jobs.

When we asked permission to suggest a plan for reorganization, the consultant agreed. We began by asking everyone to break down all the jobs that had to be done by their department. A list of fifty-two separate functions was compiled. Then we asked people to choose from that list what they *wanted* to do. The jobs were redivided among the employees, and the improvements were immediate and dramatic.

Where before there had been a great deal of mental strain and tension, the people began to truly enjoy what they were doing. And once they experienced job satisfaction for the first time, the quality of their work and their productivity skyrocketed.

Don't allow yourself to be at the mercy of your perceptions. If you don't like what you see, do something about it. Take the initiative in influencing your working and living environment. With practice, you can help determine how you see other people and how they see you.

CHAPTER 10

PERCEPTION AND MOTIVATION

"I want to build an effective team among my sales people, yet I just can't seem to keep them motivated. What would you suggest?" asked a business owner who came to my company for advice.

When we explained that motivation was something that takes on many different forms for different kinds of people, he assured us that he was attempting to treat each of his employees as individuals while trying to challenge and unite them. Yet in spite of all this, morale had become a major problem. Turnover of his key people was increasing, and nothing so far had worked in slowing the continual decline of the motivation of his sales staff.

We set up a meeting to discuss his company's needs, and the next day he gave me the tour. But I didn't need to go any farther than one of his meeting rooms. There, prominently displayed on the wall, were a number of cutouts of what appeared to be horses racing toward a finish line. Upon closer inspection, I saw that each horse had the face of one of the members of the sales staff. The "finish line" was labeled: TRIP TO HAWAII.

"So what do you think?" he asked me, beaming with pleasure that I had noticed his obviously inspired motivational tool.

"I thought you said you were treating each of your employees as individuals and trying to build a coherent team," I replied.

"Why, I am," he said, somewhat flustered. "I try all sorts of things to keep my people motivated. I think this trip to Hawaii is one of my best ideas yet. I figure it will show everybody how much I think of them even while I challenge them to be their best."

He and I then had a rather lengthy conversation about what it meant to treat people as individuals in terms of motivation and teamwork. I'm not sure I convinced him to change his tactics, but I hope I got through to him as to why some of his employees were losing morale.

Motivation Is Based on Needs

Don't get me wrong. Some people would be intensely motivated by an opportunity to win a trip to Hawaii. It would get their competitive juices flowing and challenge them to pull out all the stops in an attempt to finish the race in first place. Others, however, would be truly uncomfortable when forced to compete against their coworkers for a reward that would go to an individual rather than the group.

If it was this manager's goal to build a close-knit team, his competitive strategy was certain to backfire and would likely accomplish just the opposite effect. But he makes a good case in point: While many of us *think* we know why and how to motivate a diverse group of individuals, the task may be more complicated than we realize.

For example, a common assumption about salespeople is that they are independent, gritty, aggressive, and competitive. Most of these characteristics are probably true of a large majority of them. But even when we assemble a roomful of "independent, gritty, aggressive, and competitive" people, we must remember that each of those individuals is a unique person with a one-of-a-kind personality. Any single motivation, based on the individual, will have varying levels of success.

You might spend long hours determining which people are most similar (outwardly) in your company. You might screen out everyone else and select the most likely candidates for a special assignment. You might then create a motivational strategy based on what you have observed. Yet when you put together a group of people with very similar behaviors, you are grouping them based on their active behavior and perhaps their interests.

The problem is that effective motivation must be directed to the *needs* of people, which may have little to do with outward, active behavior. This is why a motivational approach often fails miserably. Until we learn to get beneath the behaviors of people and determine their needs, any attempt to motivate them will be hit-and-miss. Therefore, it's impossible for me to give you a "winning" motivational strategy. What motivates some people is the very thing that impedes the progress of others.

When it comes to your company, *you're* the expert. I can offer suggestions and ideas, as can thousands of other consultants, authors, and speakers. But none of us knows your people as well as you do. And since it's not possible for anyone to provide a specific strategy for motivation without interacting personally with the people involved, consider the following options.

[Note: Though the focus and applications of this chapter will dwell primarily with an employer/employee relationship, the same principles hold true for sports teams, families, members of a church congregation, and other groups. Please make the necessary adaptations.]

Back to the Components

It's no wonder that employers often miss the real needs of their employees. Needs can be so deeply hidden that even the individual is unaware of them.

You may recall that I previously listed components we use to help determine and evaluate personalities (chapter 6). Let's review those components, focusing on the need area of each one with specific regard to the issue of motivation.

Two of the components, Positive Self-Image and Need for Personal Independence, apply to any of the four colors.

Blue Quadrant

Relating to People Individually

Blue people with a strong need for close, personal relationships will be motivated by a lot of "strokes" from the boss and/or peers. He or she needs the respect of title, symbols of status, and other personalized benefits. The Blue person accepts criticism best when it is balanced with genuine praise.

Relating to People in Groups

Blue people generally have a low need for group acceptance. They're the ones who are motivated by the promise that "As long as you keep up with your job responsibilities, there's no need to attend the group scheduling and planning meetings unless you really want to." They usually thrive on opportunities to be by themselves and to work independently. While they appreciate individualized incentives and benefits, they won't enjoy them in an environment of group thinking and social pressure.

Authority Relationships

Effective motivation for Blue people requires a suggestive style of management rather than an authoritarian one. Blues thrive on individual autonomy and self-determined activities. They don't mind a formally delegated, clearly defined chain of command, but they prefer agreeable and pleasant relationships as well as the opportunity to express their real feelings and views.

Action- or Reflection-Oriented Approach

Blues with a low need for activity, but a strong need for reflection, aren't at all motivated by assignments that involve intense and prolonged physical and mental effort. They respond better when provided the opportunity to set their own pace, which usually includes plenty of time for reflective thought. They enjoy the stimulation of new ideas and procedures, and are likely to come up with original and thoughtful solutions to problems rather than taking an immediate I'll-get-right-on-it approach.

Objectivity and Subjectivity

This is the component that measures one's need to express and share strong feelings and emotions when dealing with other people. Blue people generally have a high need for empathy and want opportunities to confide their inner feelings. They prefer to deal with the relational sides of issues. They are more comfortable with familiar activities and a minimum of unexpected changes in regard to relationships. They are more motivated by personalized benefits than tangible rewards.

Making Decisions

It's important to know the amount of time needed for someone to make a decision. Blues with a high need for reflective thought do not see issues categorically, black or white. They need lots of time before having to decide on major issues. They need to think things through carefully, and perhaps to talk about their decisions with other people. Blues will generally respond well to frequent offers of assistance and friendly help.

Red Quadrant

Relating to People Individually

A Red person with a low need for individual personal relationships would be put off by the same attempts at motivation desirable for Blues. Reds much prefer a mimimum of close, personal interaction with others. They want frank and direct confrontation, correction, and instruction. It's not that they don't value praise when it is deserved, but they are not particularly motivated by titles and status as symbols of personal appreciation. They are more apt to be motivated when such perks are kept to a minimum, giving them the opportunity to focus on work, getting things done, and taking charge.

Action- or Reflection-Oriented Approach

This component deals with the amount of physical activity a person wants and needs. Reds with a high need for activity are motivated by having a "full plate" when it comes to assignments. They like having many things to do. They will appreciate any opportunity to be physically active and find outlets for their abundant energy.

Objectivity and Subjectivity

Reds with a low need for empathic relationships are better motivated by tangible benefits and advantages. They prefer to stress logic over emotion in relationships and are usually somewhat detached from the situation. Because of their matter-of-fact dispositions, they usually respond well to concrete and specific instructions and benefits.

Making Decisions

Red people are motivated by a more forceful, definite, and decisive style of supervision. They don't want to deal with shades of gray or ambiguities. They need to make quick judgments and decisions and then take immediate action.

Green Quadrant

Systems and Procedures

Green people with a low need for structure are motivated by being given a "loose rein." They don't mind following a broad schedule, but react negatively to close controls or too many details. These people have a sense of adventure and will respond well to a minimum of routine and to constant change. Making yourself readily available to them and providing them direct access to their subordinates and peers will help make them more productive.

Authority Relationships

People differ in the extent to which they need direction and control. (Remember that structure deals with rules and regulations; authority is more of a response to *personal* control.) A Green person with a high need for authority performs best for superiors and associates who are firm and forceful. He or she needs to be given opportunities to discuss and debate, and is best motivated when boundaries of authority are strictly enforced.

Teamwork and Individual Competitiveness

Greens typically have a high degree of competitive spirit as well as the need for personal advantage. A Green person with a high competitive need is the best candidate to be inspired by a "horse race" contest, where only one person will win the trip to Hawaii! Any kind of immediate reward is likely to work as a motivating factor. This person also appreciates being taken aside and assured of continual personal advancement in the company or group.

Handling Varied Assignments

Greens generally want and need variety and new experiences. Since they have a high need for change, they crave novelty and newness in each day's work. They need varied activities and a frequent change of routine.

Personal Independence

The freedom component indicates the extent to which a person likes to operate within social expectations. Greens with a high need for freedom are the nonconformists of the group. Therefore, "regular" motivation probably won't work on them. But give them assignments that allow independent action and opportunities to set their own schedule and goals, and they'll perform very well.

Yellow Quadrant

Relating to People in Groups

You will recall that this component is a measurement of a person's comfort in a group setting. A Yellow person with a high need for group acceptance would be horrified by the previously described "horse race." His or her need would be for the acceptance and support of the group. To be forced to compete against all the other "team" members would eliminate motivation rather than increase it. A much more effective motivation would be access to group encouragement and reassurance, especially during tough times.

Systems and Procedures

This is the component that measures the level of comfort with systems and procedures. Yellow people with a high need for structure are motivated when they know the organization is behind them. They want clear, spelled-out expectations, and detailed direction and guidance for how to get there. They also find consolation in the assurance of a steady and predictable income.

Teamwork and Individual Competitiveness

Yellow persons with low need for personal and competitive advantages are also people-oriented. This is not the same as the group acceptance component, which measures comfort within a group. Some Yellows are not particularly comfortable in groups, but at the same time they can still put the good of the group ahead of their own personal advancement. Regular raises, promotions, and more impressive titles won't necessarily heighten the motivation of Yellows.

They'd rather be assured that they have relationships characterized by stability and fairness. They want to know that what they are doing is important.

Handling Varied Assignments

Yellows with a low need for change are more effectively motivated when abrupt changes are kept to a minimum. They want a fixed routine and are motivated when they think things will remain the same. They will respond better if allowed to anticipate and influence change. They might also do well when you patiently help them see the larger picture of what they are doing and why some changes are necessary.

Personal Independence

People with low need for freedom need predictable situations and relationships. They appreciate order, consistency, and well-established work procedures. If you keep them informed and perhaps develop a mentor-type relationship with them, they are likely to stay motivated.

Any Quadrant

Positive Self-image

This component is something of a self-acceptance mirror, and relates to how you deal with the demands of your work or your current project. (It relates to any of the four quadrants.)

You might think people with a positive self-image would tend to be lazy or nonproductive. But in settings and on assignments suited to their relational talents and needs, they can be highly effective when they know their limitations. True, they have more need for admiration and non-punishing and emotionally protective relationships, but they can be very productive and successful. Effective motivation should come in ways that are directed to their underlying, unrecognized needs. They are likely to need help in critically evaluating their performance and mistakes.

People who are self-critical and do not have a positive self-image thrive on difficult, but definite, goals. They need personally challenging life and work situations.

Genuine encouragement is appreciated because they feel that they never accomplish quite enough. With strong and fair supervision, this person can be very productive.

So What Are Your Options?

Motivating a group of people with widely varying needs is difficult at best. Even when their needs are similar, they may be at opposite ends of the spectrum in other components. What is a manager (or a mother, a teacher, a pastor) to do?

Option #1

The worst possible option for motivating people is to set a single standard and expect it to work for everyone. Every time we focus on the needs of a single group of people, we ignore the needs of even more people. Yet how many times do we see this kind of motivational strategy being used? Salespeople can take it easy all year, yet hear of a contest during convention week and put all their energies into winning the big incentive prize. Meanwhile, a person who was really hustling all year long may observe in dismay the injustice of the system.

Teachers tend to establish a single reward system—usually one modeled after their personal preferences. But there are all kinds of students, and many become frustrated when they can't perform on a par with their peers. They can only hope that other teachers will set up a system that will acknowledge their skills and feel more natural for them.

You can probably think of countless other examples where attempts at motivation backfire. A single system of motivation usually tends to hurt more than it helps. Adult employees may be accustomed to such a structure, but we need to be careful where younger or more impressionable people are involved.

Option #2

If the worst thing we can do is set up a single standard of motivation and expect everyone to get equally excited about it, the next worst thing is to ignore the need for motivation altogether. Remember that motivation is based on *needs* of people. If *you* don't attempt to provide for them, someone else will.

Sometimes a group leader tries to remain removed from the "pack" he or she is leading, thinking that emotional distance is necessary to establish respect for the position of authority. But it is hardly a liability to respect the needs of the people who work for you (or report to you in any other setting).

It is our belief that it's important to make people feel as good about themselves as possible, that people are a company's (home's, school's, society's) most valuable asset and should be cared for emotionally as well as financially. Yet even if there were no other reason to be concerned for the personal well-being of employees, there are selfish reasons. Simply put, when needs are being met and motivation is effective, people do their best work. Turnover and low productivity are costly, while emotionally fulfilled employees are productive and profitable employees.

Option #3

As difficult as it is to identify the various needs of a diverse group of people, the best possible option is to have an objective set of scores to work with. And at the risk of sounding self-promoting, I think the questionnaire my company has created is probably the best tool you will find to take the guesswork out of assessing the behavior of employees. Our analysis separates outward behaviors from underlying needs—and it is the needs you want to deal with. The results reveal specific scores in each of the component areas. One can spot at a glance which employees are similar and which are vastly different, and what it would take to motivate each person. Effective strategies can then be designed.

Option #4

If there are no objective scores, the next best option is to discover for yourself the needs of your group. Some you can detect through observation. Others will be revealed in conversation. But the better you get to know each person, the better you will be able to determine what he or she really needs; consequently, the better you will be able to motivate the person.

With a little more attention to your group members, you will probably begin to notice patterns in what you assumed were random actions. People are driven by their needs, whether consciously or subconsciously. It doesn't take the world's best "people person" to discover the needs of others. It simply takes the will to try—and a little practice.

Option #5

When you find yourself in a position where you need to motivate people you *don't* know well, you may not be able to be specific in your strategies. But you can still apply what you know.

Since no single plan will work for everyone, experiment with a *variety* of motivational attempts. Read back through the section on components in this chapter and prepare for the vast differences you are likely to encounter. Don't limit your attempts at motivation to any single component or to one end of the scale only. Be inventive. Try several new and different motivational strategies until you find those that work with the members of your group.

In summary, remember that good leaders are good motivators. They recognize that their group members have needs. When those needs are met, the individuals will be fulfilled, productive, and happy.

If the needs go unrecognized and unmet, the individuals (and the entire group) will suffer.

Many of the needs of group members can be addressed in a work setting. It's not difficult to learn how to be a more effective leader who determines needs and learns to motivate people to ever-increasing levels of excellence. Once you know how it's done, all that's left is to *want* to do it. When you begin by motivating yourself, motivating others becomes less of a struggle.

CHAPTER 11

PERCEPTION AND VALUES

I originally gave some thought to becoming a minister—a role that has a lot to do with how a person perceives himself and the world around him. But as soon as I took my first psychology course, my career plans began to shift. I had taken only one class before World War II interrupted my schooling, but throughout the war I gave a lot of thought to perception and human behavior. When I witnessed firsthand the effects of combat stress, my interest in psychology intensified. After the war I spoke to a consultant of the Shell Chemical Company, who said that the business world was beginning to turn to psychology for help in achieving success in business. I had always been somewhat awed by the world of big business, where its leaders made major decisions every day, and I had put considerable thought into organizational leadership.

So here I was with an attraction to big business, a fascination with psychology, and a desire to minister. The result was the formation of Birkman & Associates, Inc., in which we use personality assessments to serve businesses, churches, and other organizations.

I offer this short preface to this chapter on values because I want to open with a biblical passage that has always inspired me to deeper levels of thought. Its applications affect all the areas I have mentioned—psychology, business, and ministry.

In his noted Sermon on the Mount, Jesus challenged his listeners to avoid becoming judgmental. The religious leaders of his day had constructed a complex system of rules and regulations by which "spiritual" people were expected to live. In doing so, they had circumvented much of the original intent of Scripture. They had set themselves up as models of "godliness," and they were quick to pass judgment on others.

Jesus wanted to set the record straight. First he told his listeners, in very clear terms, that they should not judge one another. Then he used this example: "Why do you look at the speck of sawdust in your brother's eye and pay no attention to the plank in your own eye? How can you say to your brother, 'Let me take the speck out of your eye,' when all the time there is a plank in your own eye? You hypocrite, first take the plank out of your own eye, and then you will see clearly to remove the speck from your brother's eye" (Matt. 7:3–5 NIV).

Jesus' questions have had a lasting impression on me. They were instrumental in my original musings about perception, and they continue to remind me of the way people tend to relate to each other.

I find it interesting that things don't seem to have changed much during the past two thousand years. I would guess that right this minute you could sit down and make a list of people with "planks" in their eyes who assume they see more clearly than you do how to run your affairs. I would imagine that such people have caused a lot of tension, if not outright conflict, for you in times past. In this chapter, I hope to show why this happens so often.

Whenever people are judgmental, it usually doesn't take long for "values" to become an issue. Yet with all the talk about values, few people clearly understand what they mean when they use the term. The issue of values is so closely related to perception that I feel we should deal with it before moving on.

What Are Values?

Defining values is not easy. Webster says vaguely that values are "a degree of excellence" or "something (as a principle or quality) intrinsically valuable or desirable." But these definitions may fall short of what we mean when we use the word.

I might go one step further and suggest that values are the high standards that influence our attitudes, behaviors, and lifestyles. But I wouldn't be surprised if you have a different definition. That's why the whole issue of *values* is so hard to grasp on a personal level, much less as a group.

Recently the issue of "family values" has been a hot political issue. Yet there was no single standard by which the term was defined, so the debate became only so much rhetoric. One side would argue that the traditional nuclear family of husband/wife/kids was the ideal model. Others countered with the argument that a single parent and child could also constitute a family unit, with an equally strong value system. Much of the issue of family *values* got lost in the confusion of family *structure*.

We should learn from this recent confusion. Whenever the topic is *values,* the term is likely to be interpreted in many ways by many people. This is a major area where people's perceptions and assumptions sometimes become very distorted. While we may not know exactly what we mean by values, most of us feel strongly about them. Perhaps it will be easier to first take a look at what values *are not* as we try to formulate a clearer picture of what they are.

Don't confuse genuine values with mere opinions.

Everyone has values. Everyone has opinions. But that doesn't mean they're the same thing. Two people with very similar values can have opinions at opposite ends of the scale. For instance, let's say two fathers are having a conversation and agree that one of the most important things in life—one of their highest values—is love for their children. They are in complete agreement on this matter.

Yet as they continue their discussion, one father believes that love is best shown by unconditional forgiveness, mercy, and vulnerability. He thinks kids will need to know that *no matter what* they do wrong, they can come to him and receive complete love and understanding.

The other father is a proponent of "tough love." Based on experiences of other parents he knows, he feels that kids need a lot of discipline. If they commit a serious offense, they should pay the penalty for it. That's the only way they will learn. If his son were arrested for drunken driving, this dad would let him spend the night in jail rather than bailing him out. It's not that he wants his children to suffer; it pains him to see them do so. But his values dictate that he take a firm hand in matters involving their welfare.

These two people can be in complete agreement at a deeper, values level. Yet the approach they take to demonstrate their values and the opinions they form along the way can be very different. If we begin to "judge" people based only on the opinions we hear them express, we may not be clear as to their actual values.

Don't confuse genuine values with poor definitions of those values.

Sometimes we know and are able to express our values with great clarity. At other times we make an honest attempt to define our values, yet don't do a very good job. And occasionally we define values with the intent of letting other people know what we expect of them.

How many times have you seen a corporate mission statement that is a complete work of fiction? A roomful of executives goes to Aruba for a week and comes back with a paragraph to dictate what the "values" of the company should be. The statement might include the following: "We value dedication and quality."

That's fine, if the corporate leaders are honest about the values they have defined. But sometimes the employees know better. They read the carefully worded statement, then they read between the lines. The *unwritten* message is: "We expect you to work long hours without complaining about your low salaries, and if you make any mistakes you can expect to be fired."

The employees may suspect, justifiably, that the first and foremost "value" of the company is making money. In some cases, business owners wouldn't care about quality of the product or emotional state of the employees if they could make a big profit. But in a competitive market, they must define their values and create certain expectations for people to follow. It's too bad when they don't really mean what they say.

Other examples are not as extreme, but follow the same patterns. We may not see any distinctions between our underlying values and the definitions we use to represent them. But if such distinctions exist, we can get confused and off-track. We need to realize that sometimes the definitions we (and others) use do not accurately reflect genuine values.

Don't confuse genuine values with your perceptions of values.

Sometimes we make assumptions about someone's values based on little more than a behavior or two we have witnessed. Previous chapters have already dealt with the problem of making assumptions based on limited perceptions, but it bears repeating here. This time try to think of some specific instances where you might be guilty of doing this.

Perhaps you see two people and think, *He's busy all the time, but she never seems to be. He's such a good worker and she's so lazy.* Your assumption *may* be correct, but not necessarily. It could be that the man is on the high end of the Activity component scale, and the woman is at the other end. Some people stay active all the time, but produce few significant accomplishments. Low-key, reflective thinkers may not show the same levels of busyness, yet can ultimately be much more productive. We aren't likely to get a good reading of work efficiency based exclusively on this single observation.

Or maybe you are in the position of hiring a new employee for your company. Two resumés stand out from the others. Both applicants have outstanding records of accomplishments, so you check their references. You ask about Liz and learn that she has a reputation for being a great team player. "I've never seen anyone so good at bringing out the best in other people," you hear. The comments about Randy, on the other hand, are more cautious. "He's something of a maverick . . . a rogue elephant. There's never been a problem with his not getting his work done, but he sure likes to do things *his* way."

For some people, that might be all they need to hear to make a decision. Many would hire Liz on the spot. But depending on the job and the needs of your company, you might be wise to interview them both and do some additional analysis. If schedules and deadlines were important to me, I'd like to know if Liz could function as well on her own as she does in a group. I'd want to know how many of her accomplishments were truly hers, and how many were team efforts. Randy is being perceived in something of a negative light, yet it seems that he still manages to get positive results with his personal style— whether other people understand him or not.

Some people would observe Liz's behavior and assume that she has a high regard for corporate values, while Randy would be seen as rebelling against those values. But that's not necessarily the case. Many people like Randy are actually more devoted to company success than people like Liz. It's just that due to his personal operating style, other people get in the way of his doing as much as he wants or needs to do. Eagles fly alone, but soar much higher than other birds. Perhaps your company really needs an eagle rather than another member of the flock.

Don't confuse values with needs.

Previous chapters have had much to say about the importance of recognizing and responding to the needs of other people. It might be natural to think that a person values all those things that he or she needs. But needs and values are very different.

The biggest difference is that we have no control over our needs. They are part of our unique and inborn personalities, neither positive nor negative. They simply exist and we must learn to deal with them. Our values, however, are *chosen*. And the values we choose may or may not correlate with our interests, needs, and other variables of personality.

For example, suppose your interests, needs, and active behavior all lie in the bottom right corner of the Life Style Grid, deep in the blue section, as far away from the other colors as possible. By nature, you would be reflective, introspective, a thinker, and a long-range planner. Yet your values might include wanting to put other people first and trying to do good things for them. You might want and need a lot of time to yourself, yet choose to join Habitat for Humanity, the organization that builds homes for people who can't afford the houses on the market. Your values might lead you to choose to develop much stronger people skills (as well as mechanical ones) that aren't part of your innate interests or needs.

Anyone observing you with a hammer in your hand and relating to people would very likely think you were doing what you liked to do. And you might indeed learn to like building houses for the disadvantaged if that's one of your stronger values. But it would take a long time for it to feel natural. You would still *need* to find plenty of time to be by yourself. Yet your values can inspire you to go beyond your natural behaviors and expressions of personality.

As you can see, it's relatively easy to talk about values, but it's also easy to confuse values with opinions, working definitions, perceptions, needs, and more. Some of us may not have any idea how to define or express our own values, yet think we know what someone else's values should be. And until I get the plank out of my own eye (clarify my perceptions), I have no right to judge another.

Our values are important for a number of reasons. First, they provide a framework for our existence. Values and philosophies of life are closely related. When we deal with age-old questions such as, "Why are we here on earth?", it doesn't take long for values to come into the picture. If one person thinks life itself is of little value and that things occur randomly and without purpose, his values would probably be quite different from someone who believes that humankind is on earth for a purpose. The second person's values are likely to reflect whatever she believes that purpose to be.

A second important function of values is to improve the quality of life. Our values rise high above our immediate (and usually more self-centered) goals and beliefs. Of course, if a person's highest value is himself and the most hedonistic lifestyle possible, then he won't see much change in the quality of his life. But most people have more altruistic values and find contentment in pursuing those higher values. Charities, churches, universities, foundations, and all kinds of other worthwhile organizations exist only through the financial support and volunteer work of people who look beyond their own concerns to the needs of others.

A third important function of values is to provide direction in life. Our values serve as a kind of filter through which we make plans and decisions. It would be a simple matter to go through life choosing whatever we want for the here-and-now. But our values have a magnetic effect. When we get to a crossroads and have to make a decision, the things we value most will usually lead us down one of the two paths at the fork. Not only do they tend to keep us moving ahead instead of merely going in circles, but they make our difficult choices a little easier to make.

As you can see, there are some pretty good reasons for knowing what our values are. Yet many people would have difficulty sitting down and writing out a definitive list. How about you? Is it time for you to give this matter some additional thought?

A Few Questions

If you need to rethink your values, or if you want to help someone else with the process, below are three questions to use as a starting point.

Where did your values come from?

Some of us may have no problem spouting off a list of values, yet would have a much harder time trying to explain *why* we believe those things or *how* they came to be. In many cases, we subconsciously adapt the value system of our families. Some of us go though life espousing "personal" values, which are actually just an echo of the things we've heard our parents say. We may or may not genuinely believe what we express as values.

As we go through life, we find other sources of help in determining our values. Some people establish higher values based on the things they come to believe at their places of worship. Some values are learned on the job. Others might be formed through contacts with schools, civic organizations, unions, etc. True values have a strong influence on individuals—one that people are likely to share with friends and acquaintances. As we interact and express our values, others may or may not choose to adopt the same standards.

As you listen to other people, there are two important things to keep in mind: (1) They might be right, and (2) They might be wrong. It's important that *you* decide what values you want to establish for yourself. If you are convinced that someone else is right, then you can alter your original views. But don't make the mistake of taking on a "herd mentality" and allowing others to do your thinking for you. One's values are too important to leave to others. This is a matter that requires *individual* thought.

It's not uncommon to have to deal with conflicting values from time to time. As we grow and begin to absorb input from more people and places, we are certain to hear opposing views—both of which may sound valid and appealing. The things we have held as values for so long may be challenged. This leads to the next question.

Do you truly believe in your stated values?

We usually discover a lack of personal commitment to our so-called values at some point in our adult lives. Some of our expressed beliefs may be challenged by college professors. We might find ourselves in moral/ethical/theological discussions, recite the things we've been told—that we *think* we believe—and quickly get shot down.

Or maybe the issue arises shortly after marriage. As two people begin to merge their individual histories of traditions and beliefs into a common tradition that both can commit to, they may have to rethink the beliefs they have always assumed to be true. And even if they get through the first few years of marriage without working out all the details, the issue will probably come up again sometime after the arrival of the first child. If Mom is passing down one set of values and Dad another, the child will be quick to notice the incongruity.

Until a situation comes along where we have to explain and/or defend our values, we probably recite what we've always been told. It's natural to assume that our parents knew what they were talking about, and they probably did. Still, they established their values using the same process—beginning with some handed-down teachings, finding the beliefs challenged by others, and making certain adjustments to determine the things they valued most. In turn, they handed those things down to us.

Are you hiding your true values for some reason?

Many people will attest to having a high value for spiritual growth and development. But based on their church attendance and time spent in individual study, you probably could never tell. Some parents insist that they value their children. At least, that's what they tell everyone at work where they spend fourteen hours a day and most weekends, leaving home before the kids are up and getting back after they're in bed!

But if you say you value something but aren't affected by it in any way, it's not a genuine value. It means nothing to claim a set of values if they aren't real. It's much better to be honest about your values and then be consistent in your pursuit of them.

For example, most people know something of how non-profit companies operate. However, other businesses (such as Christian publishing companies) are set up as for-profit companies, yet tend to see themselves as ministries. The corporate executives know that without a profit, the ministry cannot continue. And there's nothing wrong with dealing with that fact. The tendency may be, however, to "soft-sell" the need for profit to the employees. The executives may attempt to inspire and motivate the workers in terms of the people they are reaching, the need for the product, and the good they are doing rather than emphasizing profits, lest that be perceived as greedy or cold and insensitive. Therefore, they publicly hold up one set of values as more important, while making all major decisions based on the other.

It usually doesn't take the employees long to see that promotions are based on business savvy rather than a heart for ministry. Raises are awarded, not for humility and service to others, but for ability to generate profits. If the corporate leaders were more honest about their true values, then everyone in the business could work toward the same goals. It would avoid a lot of disappointment and frustration on the part of the employees, and the leaders would probably discover that few people would object to the goal of making money if they could see the corporate ministry flourish in proportion.

There can be any number of other reasons for wanting to disguise values. But until we are honest and define them clearly, we may be presenting a false picture.

Do you tend to pass judgment on the values of others?

Now we're back to someone with a plank in his eye trying to help, advise, command, or oversee someone else who has only a speck in his own eye. This problem isn't limited to spiritual settings. It happens in businesses, families, schools, and other groups every day. Often such conflicts are only a matter of perception—or misperception.

All of us can recall times when we were "the person with the speck"—facing a tiny problem, yet being given advice by pompous people who had far greater problems of their own. It's annoying and infuriating when someone else butts into our business, thinking they know what is best for us.

Yet if we're brutally honest with ourselves, we can probably recall times when we were "the person with the plank." With this hindrance to our vision, we don't "see" ourselves as pompous or annoying. We're only trying to help. But we may be insulted when the other person resists our efforts to be of assistance.

One reason conflicts arise over values is that our perceptions may not be correct. Other people don't usually mind when you disagree with them, see things from a different perspective, or hold to your own strong opinion. But to question someone's values is a serious charge. If the other person feels he or she is being judged or condemned, your relationship with that person is in serious jeopardy.

We need to understand that the other person's values may lie much closer to our own than we would ever suspect, though his or her active behavior may be just the opposite. Your needs may be different. And you may not understand what makes the person tick. But none of these things should indicate that the person lacks values.

But even if the other person *does* have different values, this doesn't mean that one set of values is superior to the other. For example, you might value spouse and family above anything and everything else. It's a noble value. Yet not everyone has a family or spouse. A single person may value his work. So during the time you devote to the kids and husband/wife, he devotes additional hours to the job, frequently choosing to work nights and weekends.

Do you instantly assume that such people are workaholics? Overly ambitious? In selfish pursuit of money and what it can provide for them? You may be right, of course. But then again, you may not be. The other person's values may be just as noble as your own. You can't always tell from a few perceptions.

Finally, let's consider a worst-case scenario. Let's suppose you know another person who *is* self-centered, greedy, and otherwise genuinely unlikable. He has no qualms about lying and cheating to get ahead, and it's obvious that his values are diametrically opposed to your own.

It is important to remember that values are chosen, so they can be changed. You have chosen your values, and even though you may envy the things this unprincipled person seems to get away with, you aren't likely to want to reject your own standards for his. Rather, try making your values clear in the hope that you may influence the person to change *his* values.

I would guess that far more of the conflicts you face on a daily basis are with people whose values are similar to your own, yet whose active behavior is considerably different. If so, it would be a shame to let the differences in personal style prevent you from working together effectively. When you hold the same or similar ultimate goals, it is imperative to see past the person's behavior to the common values you share. Otherwise, the circle of associates with whom you are comfortable is going to be severely limited.

The next chapters, dealing with spirituality and the importance of team building, will continue this theme. You'll be amazed at the difference you can see when people begin to pull together instead of pushing away from each other. This is true in personal as well as in business relationships.

One of the most important values to develop is the value of diversity. Although we're naturally drawn to people with common bonds and similarities, think how many *more* people are left out because they are different. Until we learn to value the contributions that can be made to our lives and work by different kinds of personalities, we will be the poorer.

CHAPTER 12

EYES THAT DO NOT SEE

Optional Reading

See Author's Note, Appendix 5

It's one thing to write about the connection between perception and values. But I wanted to go one step further and include a chapter on spirituality. I've seen positive results from the principles in this book evidenced in hundreds of businesses and thousands of lives. Yet the people for whom these principles work best are those who are also developing the spiritual dimension of their lives. As people discover more about themselves in relation to God, and then put what they know into practice, their lives take on a dynamic new vibrancy. As they see the truth more clearly and act on what they know, they become better managers, employees, parents, students, and husbands or wives.

The spiritual dimension of life, for me, is an invaluable source for discovering truth—and discerning what is true from what isn't. This chapter won't change anything I've written so far. Instead, it will provide some underlying reasons as to *why* I feel so strongly about these issues.

Perceiving Without Seeing

Perhaps no perception is as important as one's perception of God, because how we perceive God will strongly affect how we relate to each other. All the things we've learned about personal relationships are equally (or perhaps even more) true when it comes to a person's relationship with God. Most of us have a number of perceptions about Him from which we make assumptions. We cannot see God clearly and completely, of course, so we tend to fill in the things we don't know about Him with what we do know about ourselves. In a sense, we become guilty of creating God in our own image. If I am unsympathetic and judgmental, I am likely to assume God has those same attributes. So just as I need to separate truth from misperceptions when it comes to my business and personal life, I need to do the same with my spiritual life.

One major benefit I receive from cultivating the spiritual dimension to my life is that, while I may make the same observations as someone else, I can get a completely different perspective on what I'm seeing. This "new and improved" perspective allows me to differentiate things that are meaningless from those that are genuinely important. In addition, I begin to see people differently.

C. S. Lewis, the noted Christian writer, made a similar observation. He is quoted as saying, "There are no *ordinary* people." He goes on to explain:

> It is a serious thing to live in a society of possible gods and goddesses, to remember that the dullest and most uninteresting person you can talk to may one day be a creature which, if you saw it now, you would be strongly tempted to worship, or else a horror and a corruption such as you now meet, if at all, only in a nightmare. All day long we are, in some degree, helping each other to one or other of these destinations. . . . You have never talked to a mere mortal. . . . It is immortals whom we joke with, work with, marry, snub, and exploit—immortal horrors or everlasting splendours.[1]

Lewis knew something of perception. He perceived things beyond what he could physically see. He "saw" beyond the external appearances of other people. So should we.

If I perceive that I am supervising a group of "mere" employees, I might treat them one way. If, however, I realize that in addition to working for me, these people have lives, families, problems, souls, I might be compelled to treat them completely differently. Only with spiritual insight do I see that these people were created by God. They are loved by God. And since He values them as much as He values me, I should value them as well.

We can all modify our behaviors to some extent based on what we learn from scientific study and research. But until we get to the core of our being—the spiritual dimension—we cannot really function as we should. The difference comes from doing something you think will help your business, as opposed to doing it because you believe it is the right thing to do.

More Than Words

I believe many people give lip service to the importance of being "spiritual." It's easy to *say* the right things. Yet when observing people in a work setting, it doesn't take long to find out whether or not they truly *believe* what they say. In such an environment, one can quickly identify most of the employees who have some kind of underlying spiritual commitment. The difference is apparent in their attitudes.

I'm not talking about outward signs such as wearing religious-theme T-shirts and a cross around the neck, or putting Christian bumper stickers on cars or lockers. Rather, I refer to the deeper inner changes of people who have come to see that there is more to consider in any given situation than themselves alone. They think more broadly in terms of risks and possibilities. They see opportunities within problems. They desire friends rather than associates. They realize their weaknesses and limitations rather than egotistically insisting on their own way, trying to cover up mistakes, or blaming someone else when something goes wrong.

I want to be surrounded by people who aren't afraid to deal with truth, because a little truth almost always whets our appetite for more. For example, the more I learn about God, the better I come to know myself. And the more I discover about myself, the better I am able to see who God really is, apart from all of my previous misperceptions. It doesn't matter where I start. If I am serious about

discovering truth—either on a personal or a spiritual level—it is likely
to lead me to additional truth at other levels as well.

The Truth That Hurts Can Set You Free

We often say, "The truth hurts." But we noted in chapter 7 that
facing the truth seldom hurts as much as ignoring it. And Jesus went
one step further when He said: "You shall know the truth, and *the
truth shall make you free*" (John 8:32, italics added).

Sometimes it takes a bit of pain before freedom can be experienced.
Freedom from a toothache can require a shot of Novocaine and the
dentist's drill. Freedom from illness can require a dreaded operation.
Freedom from being out of shape and overweight requires a diet and
exercise regimen (including sore muscles and lots of sweat). Freedom
from school (graduation) requires hours of classwork, pages of homework, and the sacrifice of many hours that we'd rather be doing other
things. Yet the freedom that results in each case is well worth the
effort and pain it took to get to that point.

When dealing with perceptions, the pain we are likely to experience
before becoming free is that of facing our weaknesses. And this is
precisely where the spiritual element seems to make such a difference. People who serve God (as opposed to thinking they *are* God)
have already realized that they don't know everything. They have
submitted to a higher authority. They have come to see that only
God is omnipotent and that *they* cannot do everything equally well.

Lots of people speak of "God-given strengths." But when is the
last time you heard anyone proudly proclaiming his or her God-given
weaknesses? We take pride that God is a sovereign Creator who makes
each one of us special. As a matter of fact, we're "a little lower than
the angels . . . and . . . crowned . . . with glory and honor" (Ps.
8:5). Your specific personality is like no one else's. Yet if God gives
you a special strength in a specific area, doesn't it stand to reason
that you are created weaker in other areas? Does God see wisdom
in blending within us a sense of dignity as well as a sense of incom-

pleteness and need? Might weaknesses be assigned to each person to help us learn to trust Him?

Indeed, this concept is crucial to our spiritual development. If our reaction to weaknesses is embarrassment, fear, or shame, it will be next to impossible to cope with them. If we can't admit weaknesses, we will spend an inordinate amount of time covering them up, hiding them, or doing whatever it takes to make ourselves feel as safe and protected as possible under the circumstances.

Yet once we muster the courage to confront our weaknesses head-on, they will always point us to our strengths. You say you can't stay focused long enough to add a column of numbers the same way twice? Well, perhaps those things intruding on your concentration are ideas that could save the company money—and should be written up as proposals. Can't bear to go out on cold calls for your sales manager? Maybe that's because you're just the right person to build strong and ongoing relationships with key customers. Can't organize your sock drawer, much less the fifteen-year accumulation of junk in the garage? That's no problem if your strong point is that you're a sensitive and caring spouse. Whatever your weaknesses, you can find strengths at the opposite ends of the scales. Remember: Strengths and weaknesses are not synonymous with right or wrong. They reveal only what is right or wrong *for you.*

In addition to allowing you to discover your strengths, confronting your weaknesses also provides a sense of tremendous relief. It's as if you've been posing as Superman, only to reveal at last that you're really just Clark Kent. Even though your "secret identity" is considerably weaker than your alter ego, it feels great to let everyone know who you really are. When you admit you can no longer do everything, then—and only then—can you begin to focus on the things you like to do and are good at.

I can't help but think about the apostle Paul as this issue of weakness and strength comes to mind. If anyone was a go-getter, he was. If we were to chart Paul's usual behavior on our grid, I suspect he might show up as one of the "Reddest" characters in the Bible. There's no mistaking that he was a good people person (Green), but not at the expense of getting the job done. He was all for proper procedure (Yellow), but not at the expense of getting the job done. He was as deep and reflective a thinker (Blue) as anyone, but he still got the job done. He was almost always on the go—preaching, starting churches, writing letters from prison, or doing something to promote his faith in Jesus. He was a very strong person, yet he was well aware of his personal weakness.

Paul wrote: "There was given me a thorn in my flesh . . . to torment me. Three times I pleaded with the Lord to take it away from me. But he said to me, 'My grace is sufficient for you, for my power is made perfect in weakness.' Therefore I will boast all the more gladly about my weaknesses, so that Christ's power may rest on me. That is why, for Christ's sake, I delight in weaknesses, in insults, in hardships, in persecutions, in difficulties. For when I am weak, then I am strong" (2 Cor. 12:7–10 NIV).

Paul didn't just confront his weaknesses; he was able to boast about them. This is the importance of the spiritual element in the workplace (and elsewhere): It provides me with strength that is not my own. I may feel weak and perhaps even incompetent from time to time. But my weaknesses point to my strengths. They also point to One from whom I can find additional strength.

Our Mentor Who Art in Heaven

So the cycle begins as I confront my personal weaknesses. But soon I may discover another problem. When I begin to see more clearly who I am and discover God as a source of strength (an ally rather than an opponent), I may see that I have developed some serious misperceptions about Him. Perhaps I've been blaming Him for my weaknesses so long that now I'm not sure how to relate to Him. Perhaps I've accused Him of being judgmental, vindictive, insensitive to my needs, disinterested, or any number of other things. Or maybe I feel that I've hurt God's feelings in the past, which has created a reluctance to turn to Him now.

If so, am I in for a surprise! When at last I become open to a spiritual relationship, I find out how wrong I may have been. Or more likely, I find out that while many of my perceptions of God have been correct, the overall picture is still very much incomplete. Certainly God is all-powerful. He does act as judge, frowning on the things I have done wrong in my life and/or business. Any moral and ethical shortcuts I've taken in the past may have bothered me a bit, but they bothered God even more.

Yet as I seek to turn things around, I discover that God is not only fair, but merciful as well. He is Judge, yes, but He is also Savior. He knows everything I've done wrong, but He's waiting, eraser in hand, to hear my confession and wipe the slate clean. I begin to see all those attributes I've assigned to Him from my own personal inadequacies (insensitivity, vindictiveness, and such) as the misperceptions they are. I find that even my worst behavior can be forgiven as He calls me back into a rich and meaningful relationship with Him.

So when I learn the truth about myself, I see God more clearly. When I see God more clearly, I discover more about myself. The cycle of spiritual development continues.

One way I like to think of God is in terms of a mentor. Many business consultants recommend that leaders at all levels find mentors who can both train them and set a good example. We go to our mentors for advice, for help with our struggles, for affirmation, for companionship, and more. We learn to be completely open and honest when we speak to them about our feelings. Otherwise, how can they help us?

The same types of things a mentor can do for us on a business level, God can do on a spiritual level. I go to Him with my problems, and He can provide peace, if not immediate answers. I share my victories with Him and feel more fulfilled. When I let Him in on my emotional state of mind—even if I'm angry or confused about *Him*—I am usually able to see a different perspective on the situations I face. With God as my mentor, I can maintain a sense of balance I am otherwise unable to achieve.

I think it's true to say that I need God's help more at work than I do at church or other "spiritual" places and times. Since I regard church as a protected environment, I believe more "spiritual warfare" is done in business hallways and boardrooms than in most sanctuaries. It's not that churches aren't doing their job. It's just that we "warriors" are more isolated and outnumbered after we get to work. It is in the "real" world where I face more stress, temptation, risk, failure, judgmental attitudes, and other things for which I need help from God, the Mentor.

Take Another Step

Even after I begin to see myself more clearly and to see God more clearly, there is another step I need to take. In the dozens of human interactions I have each day, many of the people with whom I come in contact may not have discovered as much about themselves (or God) as I have. They may be the way *I* used to be—self-centered, insecure, afraid to admit weaknesses. The next step is for me to become more of a positive influence on them than I allow them to become a negative influence on me. If spiritual principles do not apply to practical, everyday experiences, what good are they?

Jesus told a story about a Pharisee—an extremely well-educated religious teacher—and a tax collector who was no more popular in his day than his counterparts are today. The point Jesus makes should apply to every parent, business executive, and any other person who recognizes the need to set an example for others. Here's the story:

> Two men went up to the temple to pray, one a Pharisee and the other a tax collector. The Pharisee stood and prayed thus with himself, "God, I thank You that I am not like other men—extortioners, unjust, adulterers, or even as this tax collector. I fast twice a week; I give tithes of all I possess." And the tax collector, standing afar off, would not so much as raise his eyes to heaven, but beat his breast, saying, "God, be merciful to me a sinner!" I tell you, this man went down to his house justified rather than the other; for everyone who exalts

himself will be abased, and he who humbles himself will be exalted (Luke 18:10–14).

This short parable speaks to me on many levels. First, it shows that a little spirituality can be a dangerous thing. The Pharisee seemed to think he had reached a spiritual destination, yet the quest for genuine spirituality is a *continual* journey.

Second, it is better to know one thing and put it into practice than be a know-it-all without any attempt to *apply* the knowledge. Fasting, giving, and other spiritual disciplines do little good if they have no effect on the person's attitude.

Third, and to me most important of all, is that probably everyone who witnessed this scene described by Jesus would have been deceived by their perceptions. Put yourself in that scenario as an observer. You would see two people: one, a self-confident religious teacher who by his own admission thought he was doing an excellent job at handling his life; the other, a confessed sinner. Whom would you have chosen as the better model? Which of the two would you employ? Which one would you seek out as a coworker?

I hope by this point in the book you know to identify a person's socialized behavior and look beyond it, but old habits are hard to break. I must admit, the Pharisee *looks* like the better risk, though he had a lot of people fooled. Most of us wouldn't have given the other guy a second glance. Only God had the wisdom to detect the arrogance of the Pharisee as well as the potential of the tax collector.

Two questions come to mind at this point: (1) To what extent have I become a Pharisee; and (2) To what extent am I being deceived by the Pharisees that surround me? If I'm a parent, am I trying to teach my kids one set of values while modeling the opposite? If I'm an employee of whom a great deal is expected, can I discern whether my boss has the company's best interests at heart or is simply trying to make himself look good? If I'm a CEO, have I turned the management of my company over to a managerial level of smart-looking, smart-talking Pharisees who care little for customer needs and even less for the employees they oversee?

For me, having a spiritual dimension helps at both levels. I first become willing to see myself as I really am and make the changes I need to make. I then begin to perceive others much more clearly and deal with any well-disguised hypocrisy or other Pharisee-like behavior that threatens my company or coworkers.

I'm assuming that most of us don't want a company made up of Pharisees, a classroom of Pharisees, or a home full of Pharisees. Personally, I'd much rather work with raw individuals who are eager to change for the better than a group of "pros" who are convinced they have nothing more to learn.

Change is risky. Change can be painful. And change is never a sure thing. But as a goal or philosophy of action, change is usually the best option. The only alternatives are stagnation in one form or another. I believe most people want change, yet are very much afraid of it. It's back to the issue of facing weakness and pain. The tax collector surely didn't enjoy his bitter confession and repentance, but it was a more effective and lasting action than the Pharisee's hollow words.

What Are You Searching For?

I look to the Bible as a source of authority and truth. It is filled with many excellent lessons about perception, especially in regard to spirituality. I have already referred to a couple of examples, but I would like to offer one more.

We may think that Jesus came down hard on the people who rejected Him, but He was actually just as concerned (if not more so) that the people *close* to Him learn something. At one point after His disciples had been following, listening to, and observing Him for quite a while, He wanted to give them a serious warning that would save them a lot of grief in the future. However, they were still quite dense when it came to spiritual enlightenment and they completely missed His point. He paused mid-lecture and asked them: "Do you still not see or understand? Are your hearts hardened? Do you have eyes but fail to see, and ears but fail to hear?" (Mark 8:17–18 NIV).

In my dealings as a business consultant, I have seen many pairs of "eyes that fail to see." (What a good metaphor for us as students of perception!) The business owner and I can be looking at the same staff, the same personnel, the same spreadsheets, and the same statistics. But while I see opportunity, he sees problems, despair, apathy, or worse.

You might ask: "What, exactly, is it that some people can see that others can't?" In a word, "Hope"—but not a baseless, pie-in-the-sky kind of hope. It's a hope based on confidence in our Christian faith. It's the kind of hope that allows me to make decisions and move on when I'm not completely sure of myself. It's the kind of hope that gives me the courage to act on my convictions when it seems a lot "safer" to take questionable shortcuts. It's the kind of hope that says, "Yes, I *can* handle the stresses and strains of running a business, being a good parent, or whatever else I have to do."

Most of us have felt hopeless at times. Our spiritual eyes have failed to see. But if we blink a couple of times and readjust our spiritual perceptions, we can begin to perceive more clearly who God really is. Hopelessness dissipates as we see that we can place our hope in a God of love, forgiveness, and strength.

Oh, By the Way . . .

Whenever I bring up the topic of spirituality, a question usually arises: "Do you detect a noticeable difference in the way the different 'colors' of the Life Style Grid go about dealing with spiritual matters?" I usually hesitate to answer because our research is by no means qualitative. We've had people volunteer to respond to questions, but the research is already somewhat skewed because of the higher percentages of outgoing Greens and deep-thinking Blues who are likely to participate.

However, we do seem to get a few fairly clear patterns—at least, in regard to the potential problem areas. As stated previously, we tend to fill in whatever we don't know about someone with what we *do* know to be true about ourselves. Red-quadrant individuals are take-charge people by nature, so they tend to see God as a God of *action*. They perceive Him as strict, and their obedience may be motivated more by obligation than privilege. Also, the "have-to-win" attitudes of some Reds may make submission to God more difficult than for others.

The Yellow-quadrant people feel compelled to do everything just right. So when the issue is a serious matter like spirituality and one's relationship to God, many of them feel a lot of stress. The Pharisees we've been talking about demonstrate Yellow behavior to the extreme. They focus on the rules and regulations of their religion, and completely miss the big picture. Yellows may need more help focusing on the personal relationship with God rather than do's and don'ts.

Green-quadrant people are just the opposite. They tend to focus too heavily on the relationship. They are the people most likely to trivialize the holiness of God with a "Big Guy in the Sky" or "God, My Good Buddy" mentality. They reflect the same desire to win demonstrated by the Reds, but the Green people want to win in order to be liked by others. If not careful, they project a performance-oriented routine with shallow roots into actual spiritual knowledge.

And finally, the Blues see God more in conceptual terms. The ongoing introspection that takes place in their minds never allows them to completely understand Almighty God. But that doesn't keep them from trying. Blues are heavy in attendance at religious seminars, many of them becoming seminar addicts. They frequently need help in taking action based on what they *do* know about God rather than accumulating additional insight into His nature.

The challenge for *all* of us is to attempt to "see" more clearly (in terms of spiritual perception) than we have in the past. Spiritual 20/20 vision may not be possible with earthly eyes, but clearer perception and subsequent personal improvement *is*. May we all become people of vision.

---

[1]C. S. Lewis, *The Weight of Glory and Other Addresses* (New York: Macmillan, 1980).

CHAPTER 13

BUILDING EFFECTIVE TEAMS

If you played some kind of organized team sport as a child or were a member of a gym class that included such sports, you probably received instruction on the importance of teamwork. You were taught to work toward common goals and to put forth your best individual effort for the good of the team. You were proud to wear the Little League uniform, the school jacket, the band colors, or the appropriate insignia of your team.

Later in life, however, many of us lose sight of the importance of teamwork. Perhaps we simply have fewer opportunities for team involvement. But more likely the former focus on the good of the team is replaced with subtle teachings on how to "get ahead," how to "maximize your potential," or how to "look out for number one." Individual achievement becomes the ultimate goal, and life too often becomes a competitive event rather than a team effort.

A successful life, however, will consist of both individual effort *and* devotion to a larger team. At an address given at Edinburgh University, Sir Alexander Fleming said, "It is the lone worker who makes the first advance in a subject: the details may be worked out by a team, but the prime idea is due to the enterprise, thought and perception of an individual." He was aware of both the independent and team efforts necessary to get things done.

Our society tends to recognize individuals rather than teams. As a result, we may be tempted to "solo" more often than we should when we would do much better in the context of a cohesive group. We need to recognize the efforts of others who contribute to our individual successes. Sir Isaac Newton did. Even though he was recognized and credited for many achievements during his lifetime, he once wrote to Robert Hooke, a fellow English scientist, "If I have seen further [than others], it is by standing upon the shoulders of giants." Newton recognized that his own independent accomplishments were only possible because of those who had gone before him.

We should be just as gracious in recognizing our own team support in whatever we do. We also need to acknowledge the teamwork behind many of the individuals we have lauded. For example, Christopher Columbus gets a lot of credit for discovering the new world. But he didn't sail all three ships. Who were the other brave captains? What about all the frightened crew members who risked falling off the edge of the world to make possible such a voyage? Columbus wasn't even correct in his assumptions of where his trip would take him. Yet he is singled out for fame and recognition, while most people can't tell you another person who was included on any of his expeditions.

You may not be making headlines, but from time to time you are going to be put in the spotlight for the good things you do. Are you going to take all the credit, or will you remember the team members who helped you get there?

Even famous teams are sometimes guilty of leaving out important members. Meriwether Lewis and William Clark are one of American history's most noted examples of teamwork. Yet they might still be going around in circles if not for the help of Sacajawea, their Shoshone guide and interpreter. Rodgers and Hammerstein surely had other musical influences, as Currier and Ives likely had artistic ones. The achievements we call "ours" are almost always based on other team players, past or present.

We never stop being part of a team, though after childhood, most of us cease to wear uniforms and other paraphernalia that associate us with specific groups. (Notable exceptions are military personnel and professional sports teams.) We move on from our organized groups and teams and confront life on our own. But whether or not we realize it, we still belong to a number of "teams."

Team Preparation

John Donne's observation holds true: "No man is an island, entire of itself." And since we are incapable of being our own little islands, we should stop trying so hard to separate ourselves from the rest of the world. Few of us are capable of, or desire to, live as hermits. Most of us want and need human interaction. We usually accept the bonds that come naturally. But the next and more important step is to seek out other opportunities to form teams that may have previously been overlooked.

Below are a few things to keep in mind about team building before we actually get into the how-to's that are involved.

For the most part, life is a team effort.

Sometimes you discover "team members" in unusual or unexpected places. Even orders of monks who seek seclusion and silence do so in groups. Rather than become "islands," they compose a team where everyone contributes to the good of the whole. Similarly, we all have teams to which we belong. A team can be a family, a work group, a social club, a neighborhood, a church, or any group of people who interact on a regular basis.

Most of us probably spend considerably more time with our teams than we do alone. That's one reason why it's so important to learn to build *effective* teams. Since we're going to be in so many groups anyway, we may as well try to make the most of the time we spend together.

The stronger our teams, the better our quality of life.

Team involvement includes both advantages and disadvantages. Once people have identified and begun to associate with their fellow team members, they begin to accept the responsibility of caring for one another. When one of them is temporarily weak or otherwise incapacitated, the other team members can support him or her and carry on. It is a good feeling to know that, if we're forced to stop or slow down for a while, everything will not come to an end.

On the other hand, being part of a team means we don't always get to do what *we* want to do. And even when we do, it may not be exactly *when* we had hoped to do it. Team commitments will occasionally conflict with individual desires. In such cases, one's personal plans must sometimes be put on hold to keep the team moving ahead. When teams are working together and making progress toward a common goal, the enthusiasm and optimism is contagious. It's a joy to be involved. Few things in life are as fulfilling as being part of a dynamic team—whether at home, at work, in sports activities, in service organizations, or anywhere else.

On the other hand, when you don't enjoy being with the people you *have* to be with, the quality of your life can take a steep nosedive. Ask anyone who wakes up every morning with nothing but a feeling of dread about having to go to work. Or ask a teenager whose parents are continually bickering with each other and taking their frustrations out on *him*. Whenever "teams" don't develop teamwork, and they're forced to spend a lot of time together anyway, they are perpetually uncomfortable and frustrated.

Most teams won't get stronger unless someone takes the initiative.

Have you ever been in a group where no one really seemed comfortable because nobody appeared to know what was going on? Meetings are scheduled, the "team" assembles, yet no one seems to take any responsibility for bringing group members closer together. In many cases, all it would take is for one person to be willing to start asking questions, initiating conversation, and beginning to make team members more comfortable with each other.

Even within families, PTA meetings, social clubs, or other informal groups, one person can make a major difference. If no team builders are designated, someone needs to assume the role. It usually takes a minimum of effort to accomplish a significant amount of team building. But it won't happen until someone wants it to happen and does something about it.

Team Participation

The following suggestions should work, whether you're a CEO trying to assemble the best possible management team or a parent attempting to bring harmony to a turbulent family. Some of these ideas should sound familiar by now, since they're based on principles already discussed in this book. But almost everything that has been said so far applies in some way to team building. The better we learn to interrelate through improved perceptions and understanding of various behaviors and personalities, the more ease we will have in forging the strongest possible teams.

Learn to value diversity.

Let's start by repeating the statement at the end of the last chapter: It's one thing to be aware that people are different, but if we want to put together a good team, we're going to need to *value* those differences. We all like to think that we're smart enough to know what's best in most situations, and we tend to form models of excellence based on our own scintillating personalities. It works for us, so we expect other people to conform.

But let's suppose you put together a team of people exactly like yourself. Would you anticipate any problems? Certainly all your strengths would be multiplied by the number of people on the team, but then, so would your weaknesses. No one would be there to take care of all those necessary functions that you detest so much, and the whole team would suffer for it.

One of the functions of valuing diversity is to *protect* it. If you are the person responsible for assembling the team, suppose you have gathered together all kinds of personalities and have all your bases covered. Even at that point your job is by no means finished, however.

What will happen is that the Reds and Greens will quickly start talking, since that is their natural, active behavior. The quieter and less direct Yellows and Blues will start thinking about the issues. But if you don't watch out, the Reds will have a solution they're ready to implement before the Yellows or Blues have even had an opportunity to speak up. It won't necessarily be the best solution, but they'll be ready to roll with it.

You (or some designated team leader) will need to ensure that input is received from all team members. It won't be a problem with some of the people involved, but others will need time and encouragement to put their thoughts together and open up. Yet in most cases, you'll be glad you waited to hear what they have to say, as they will see the issue from a completely different perspective and will raise the right questions at an early enough stage to prevent you from wasting time and money in pursuing a less effective course of action.

The people least like you are probably the very ones you need most.

We can't say we value diversity and then rule out certain kinds of people from the team. If you're an aggressive, go-getter kind of person, you may not understand at all the personality of a quiet, reflective planner. But you need that person on your team. If you are a persuasive talker, you have no idea what makes those numbers-oriented accounting people tick. But you'd better put one of them on the team.

Doesn't it make sense that the reason you simply can't figure out certain people is because your weaknesses are their strengths, and vice versa? They operate in a completely different manner from you. When you're working independently, these people always seem to impede your progress by wanting seemingly useless information and making strange requests. You can put them off until you have time to deal with them. But to put them on a team? To meet with them on a regular basis and *ask* for their opinions?

It's a strange and symbiotic relationship, but you need each other. Those people need your specific strengths, and you need theirs. The fact that you are so different is the very reason you need to interrelate. And even while people who are in diagonally opposite corners of the Life Style Grid are trying to figure each other out, they will find themselves helping to interpret for people in the other two colors who are also at odds. But once communication involving all four quadrants begins, you will see previously unimagined opportunities, options, potential problems, and all sorts of other insights. As hard as it might be to include certain kinds of people on your team, you will have an even harder time trying to solve problems or make plans *without* them.

Good teams allow everyone the freedom to maintain active behavior.

Not only do you need to value the diversity of your team members, they need to value *each other's* diversity. That means that during brainstorming sessions, some people are likely to form a group and begin to feed off of each other's ideas. Others will sit alone and write out their ideas. Some may sit there with their eyes closed for long periods of time. But if this is how they operate best, they should be encouraged to do so. If they all try to do things the same way, many of them will feel uncomfortable and will not be nearly as productive.

It may seem a bit strange at first to allow such a diversity of behaviors among the same team, but soon it will become a freeing sensation. As people observe that others have the freedom to be themselves—no matter how unorthodox their methods—observers will be more willing to express their own styles. And when people become comfortable in a group setting, the possibilities are almost unlimited.

Good teams produce synergy.

Synergy occurs when a variety of elements combine to cause a greater effect than the sum of their individual parts. Teams are important because they allow knowledgeable and creative individuals to interact with each other. When the ideas and communication begin to flow, the results can be amazing.

You may have witnessed a similar phenomenon in sports. For example, I used to be an avid tennis player (when I still had the knees for it). Most tennis players will attest to the fact that their games improve significantly when playing an opponent who is considerably better. This is not exactly logical. You would think that you would play better against someone with approximately equal or lesser skills. Yet when allowed to interact with a person of greater skill, something happens to inspire less experienced players to perform at a higher level.

You may have some people who excel at independent achievement. They may not enjoy or appreciate groups in general. Yet if you assemble the right team, even your most productive people should become more challenged and motivated. More than likely, they detest groups that waste time or opportunities. But those groups are in no way "teams," at least not by my definition.

Effective teams will bring out the best in all the members—even those who by nature are loners. A good team should have something to offer everyone.

Teamwork should never be equated with committee work.

Teams should not (and cannot) function with the expectation that the group will do the work of each of the individuals. Most of us have been on committees where nothing was ever done because decisions were never made until group consensus was reached.

On an effective team, however, each person should be responsible for whatever he or she does best. Those responsibilities are not relegated to the team as a whole. The other team members are there to provide input, alternative options, to alert them to potential hazards that should be considered, etc. In a team setting, such matters can be dealt with quickly and efficiently. Members act as sounding boards for all the other members, but the individuals are not deprived of their power to move ahead with their own decisions.

The better team members know each other, the more smoothly this process will go. One good example is the field of publishing. Various people have very specific responsibilities, yet they must work together as a team. The author (usually a quiet and introspective type of person) has creative ideas to share. The editor (whose people skills are important) knows what the market is looking for and helps the author shape the manuscript into the best possible form. The proofreader (who must be good with details and procedures) ensures that nothing is out of order when the manuscript is complete. And the publisher (who ultimately wants to make money from this whole process) turns the marketing staff loose with their skill and experience in selling, advertising, and promotion.

Each of these areas requires a very specific kind of person with unique talents. But all of them must depend on each other to see that the job is done well. The better they know each other and the roles each person is to play, the better they will function as a team. When the author learns more about the market and does a better job of targeting the book for a specific group, the editor has more time to "fine-tune" the content. When the salespeople know the author better, they can create better strategies and campaigns. And on it goes.

Team members retain the responsibility for getting done what needs to be done. But on a functioning team, each person's skills are enhanced by the input and assistance of the other members.

Teams must be created, not expected to evolve.

Sometimes we are amazed to see teams come together naturally, with little or no planning. But if and when this occurs, someone needs to analyze the situation and make sure the team is as strong as it should be.

It may be like having a boat that looks absolutely gorgeous on shore. The engine purrs like a kitten. The brass railings are polished and glowing. The hull is freshly painted. The wood is in excellent shape. The galley is well-stocked. The boat is the envy of everyone who walks by. Yet as you gently place the boat in the water, you become aware of a small leak. You must tend to the leak, or all the other preparation will have been in vain.

Sometimes a team will "spring a leak." The holes may be tiny and imperceptible at first. Indeed, if it had been a gaping hole, it would have been noticed and attended to right away. But a team can "sail" for quite a distance before any small holes are discovered. And when the ship is far from shore, it can be most inconvenient to begin bailing and trying to plug leaks.

Whenever a team is formed, examine it for "holes" immediately. Do you have a numbers cruncher? A long-range planner? A person who can sell the ideas to the right people? A person who can create new and different options from existing plans? All of these people need to be involved from the first—to get to know each other and take ownership of the team's group efforts. Don't let needs go unattended for too long.

Advanced Team Building

At this point I could reiterate much of the material already covered in this book. I could remind you that your way of doing things is not necessarily the only way, nor even the best way. I could warn you again not to evaluate other team members based only on their behaviors, because valid interaction involves consideration of their interests and needs. Instead, I will only encourage you to review the previous chapters and make your own applications to team building. Keep in mind at all times that when one team member suffers, everyone suffers. Similarly, when one person excels, the whole team looks good.

I also need to clarify that the means of team building discussed so far have been described in terms of what *anyone* can do. It takes a bit of common sense, understanding of human nature, and perseverance to make it through the initial rough spots, but almost any "amateur" can learn to build a strong team. Yet sometimes the situation calls for a bit more preplanning.

For example, in companies where teams of high-paid executives are being put together, I would strongly suggest investing in a professional consultant for evaluation. When the team builder has access to a set of scores for all his prospective members, the task of putting together the right people and filling all the holes is made considerably simpler. He or she knows what to look for in advance. While it is possible to go a long way on instinct and observation alone, human beings are so complex that it is very difficult to assemble just the right combination of personalities to accomplish complex jobs in the best possible manner. You wouldn't want to duplicate certain skills or to overlook others.

One case in point is a hotel chain that called my company for advice with a problem they had not been able to solve: The executive staff just couldn't get along. They had tried all kinds of motivations and even a change of personnel, but nothing seemed to work. The people stayed at each others' throats all the time. They wanted us to see if we could do some team building in the midst of all the discord.

First, we asked everyone to fill out our questionnaire so we could get some scores and have a place to start. We sat down and evaluated the component scores, explaining the difference between active behavior and reactive behavior. There were audible sighs and frequent "Aha's" throughout the room.

When we investigated the strong response to the scores, we discovered that the hotel industry is an extremely high-stress vocation. We found that every person who had filled out the questionnaire was usually in reactive behavior while at work—acting out of stress rather than a natural, effective operating style. Many of the people had worked together for five years *and had never witnessed each other's active, normal behavior.*

One person had been generally detested for pestering them for reports when they were busy with other duties. As it turned out, he explained that he had been covering for them with upper management. He had demanded just enough from them to keep their superiors happy and thought he deserved praise for his efforts rather than scorn. After he opened up, everyone else began to share their own concerns and committed to try to help each other stay in active behavior as much as possible. As soon as they realized that they had been seeing only the worst in each other, they decided to search for the *best*.

Team building is not always easy, but it's almost always worth the effort. The investment of time and energy will result in better communication, increased productivity, and happier, more stress-free working conditions for all.

CHAPTER 14

CLOSING CHALLENGES

In trying to think of an appropriate way to summarize all the things I have been trying to communicate in this book, I am reminded of Hans Christian Andersen's *The Emperor's New Clothes*. We all know the story of the leader who was willing to parade naked down the street as crowds watched, rather than be honest and admit that he couldn't see something he *should* have been able to see. Talk about a problem with perception!

We never outgrow the charm of such fairy tales. Nor the truth! For why else would these tales be so enduring (and endearing) if they didn't "hit home" for so many of us? Don't you know people who go to ludicrous extremes to defend themselves if their integrity is questioned in any way? Haven't you ever caught yourself going along with a group decision when you didn't actually believe it was the wisest course of action? And aren't there times when situations get so complicated that you'd give anything to be the one to stand with childlike innocence and proclaim, "The emperor has no clothes"?

Unfortunately, most of us learn to divert our eyes from such garish and embarrassing truths and do whatever it takes to fit in. Maybe we're too intimidated by the "emperor" in charge to speak up and point out that something is amiss. Perhaps we've tried to speak the truth in the past, and have been chastised for it. It could be that we're too insecure to express a minority opinion among a group of people who seem to agree that the glaring problem in front of them doesn't actually exist.

While the emperor would have done better to confront the truth and cover up a little, the majority of us need to confront the truth and *uncover* ourselves rather than hiding who we really are. If we do, we'll never gather accurate perceptions and information about each other. And until we become a bit more vulnerable and willing to be our true selves, we won't be able to accomplish any of the challenges set forth in this book.

None of these principles are difficult or a chore. Far from it. When you learn to be yourself and quit trying to behave like someone else or perform to some unspecified standard, nothing will seem easier or more therapeutic. What's *unnatural* is to go through life unsure of your own skills, style, or personality. Consider these final challenges.

Start Now to Avoid Future Misperceptions

What we know we should do and what we actually choose to do are sometimes very different. That's why fairy tales still appeal to us. In our minds we know that we should never be afraid to speak the truth (even to an emperor), that we should be kinder to the warty frogs we meet, that some of the ugliest beasts we know have the strongest passion for beauty, and that we all want to live happily ever after. But in *real* life, we don't always act on what we know and believe.

I would challenge you right now to begin to see other people with a deeper degree of sensitivity and understanding than ever before. Even those you traditionally write off and ignore might become close allies if you get to know them better. But you have to get past those initial erroneous assumptions you're making based on too few perceptions.

When people do something that annoys you, don't be so quick to take it personally. You might be making wrong assumptions based on their actions. They may have a completely different style of behavior—one that's just as valid as your own. They may be under stress and operating out of their reactive behavior. If you misread someone's actions and eliminate any further desire to know them better, it will ultimately be your loss.

You may agree with me 100 percent. But until you start—right now—to see past any potential problems with the behavior of other people, that knowledge won't do you any good. You must apply what you know, or this book will be of no more use to you than a doorstop or a fireplace starter.

Accentuate the Positive

As much as possible, emphasize a person's strengths. Personalities aren't a matter of right or wrong and good or bad. In all the scales we use for our components of personality, both ends indicate certain strengths. People in the center have a combination of those strengths. In some cases, those strengths will cause them to excel. In others, they won't be as valuable. But they're still strengths.

Part of understanding what has been written in this book is adapting a more positive outlook toward other people. As long as we evaluate others according to our own standards and expectations, we impede effective communication and development of relationships. When we begin to comprehend that everyone has positive and unique strengths to bring to any situation, we find a new depth of understanding.

I would challenge you to think of three specific people whom you don't naturally get along with. These should be people who aren't blatantly evil or despicable, but those with whom you never seem to see eye-to-eye. Go through the steps of trying to identify their interests, active behaviors, needs, and reactive behaviors. Determine what color(s) they would fit in the Life Style Grid. Create a list of ideas on how to communicate with them more effectively. Then, when the time is right, actually try some of these ideas.

If it works with one or more of the three people you have chosen, move on to others, working to perfect your strategies. Everyone has strengths and admirable qualities tucked away in their personalities, even if it's hard to see past the outer shells. They may seem hard-nosed, obnoxious, apathetic, self-absorbed, or worse. If so, you have to play the role of detective. Take your magnifying glass of understanding and go in search of clues as to the positive aspects of their personalities. A good detective will uncover an impressive body of evidence to show that the person is indeed a worthwhile and valuable individual underneath the facade he or she happens to be displaying at the moment.

Let the "Real You" Show Through Your Socialized Behavior

Even if you can't crack the shell of other people, no one is stopping you from cracking your own shell from the inside. Eliminate all false behaviors. Sure, you still want to impress your boss. Yes, some situations call for conforming to a certain code of behavior. But there's much you can do to reveal your true self to others most of the time.

Stop talking about the boss's interests for a while (out of habit, to impress him) and share some of your own instead. If everyone else is getting too intense in a meeting, don't get sucked into the conflict. Use your unique sense of humor to lighten the atmosphere. When opportunities arise to let down your guard and give others a clear glimpse of who you really are, take advantage of them.

Somewhere, tucked away among all those "proper" and "expected" things you do is a one-of-a-kind personality that, like Cinderella's slipper, doesn't fit anyone except you. Until you learn to wear your unique personality with pride, you won't be happy or comfortable. And if you aren't happy with who you are, no one else is likely to be, either.

Step Back and Get a Different Perspective

Do you remember the story of the five blind men and the elephant told in chapter 1? The moral of that story seems to have come full circle. I want to remind you, just before ending this book, that some-times we become too accustomed to the situations we find ourselves in or too close to our problems to perceive them clearly. Perhaps you've seen intense magnifications of common objects. You might be looking at a butterfly wing, a flower petal, or a portion of the "Mona Lisa." But by the time the image has been magnified several thousand times under the lens of the microscope, it appears monstrous and threatening.

We need to occasionally retreat from the things that cause us so much aggravation. We need to go far away and get a completely different perspective. Rather than magnifying the problem under a microscope and seeing it at its worst, we need to stand so far away that we must use a telescope to see it at all. From that view, the problem no longer seems large and looming. Instead, it seems small and insignificant. And from our distant vantage point, we can see past the problem to the bigger picture. Then we can make wiser, more relaxed, decisions about coping with the issue.

Some people, when too close to their problems, become frozen, transfixed, like a deer caught in the glare of headlights. While we can't ignore our problems or take them too lightly, neither should we take them so seriously that we're immobilized. Sometimes the best way to move forward is to take several steps backward and get a new and refreshing perspective.

Try Some Different Lenses

We tend to condemn the naiveté of people who look at the world "through rose-colored glasses." The phrase, of course, refers to the desire of some people to overlook obvious problems and see only the positive side of things. Being optimistic is one thing, but refusing to deal with reality is another. Yet I would encourage you to try some different colored lenses. If by nature your interests, behaviors, and needs lie in the Yellow portion of the Life Style Grid, then I hope you will occasionally attempt to see the world through the lenses of a Red person. Then try the view from the perspective of a Green and then a Blue. I'm not suggesting that you attempt to change your own personality or alter your behaviors, yet you can gain tremendous insight by going through a portion of a day trying to see the world from someone else's perspective.

The insight you gain will help you understand other kinds of people better. You should begin to see that their personalities and methods are just as valid as your own. In addition, you should begin to see that your own place on the "team" is more essential than you might have thought. What would all those other people do without the skills that you bring to the mix? And what would *you* do without *theirs?*

I sincerely hope that some of the things in this book will make a difference in your life. And I hope even more that you'll begin to incorporate the things you've learned into your perceptions and relationships.

If you're in the Red quadrant, you probably won't even still be reading! When you came to the first suggestion or idea you thought would work, you probably went out to implement it. May you have great success. (Eventually, I hope you find your way back to the book and additional ideas that will be of help to you.)

If you're in the Yellow quadrant, you'll probably want to put a specific plan together before you move ahead. Perhaps you'll assign chapters 4 through 6 to be read by Wednesday and discussed at a meeting in Conference Room B from 9:30 till noon where coffee and cheese danish will be served unless it rains, in which case another plan will be provided. That's fine too. The better you construct a plan that works for you, the more you'll get out of the material presented.

The Green-quadrant people will tend to congregate and talk about the content of the book. They'll discuss it with each other, and they'll tell their friends what they've been reading. This may go on for quite a while . . . perhaps until a Red person comes along and helps show them some ways to take a hands-on approach to the material. But if they like what they have read, a lot of other people are likely to hear about it.

And you Blues—the ones after my own heart—aren't going to do anything for a while. You're going to mull the new ideas over to determine whether or not you really agree with them. You'll combine them with other concepts you've been dwelling on lately. You'll muse, conjecture, and put some deep thought into what you've read. And eventually you'll hit upon just the right plan to help yourself or your group succeed in the long run. I hope some of the things in this book have helped inspire you to a level of deep thinking.

What I hope you *won't* do is say, "Pretty good book," and stick it back on the shelf with all the others you've read. At least, not before you begin to use some of the concepts to your advantage. Some books don't need too much thought or application. Some present a premise that you either agree with or don't. Some deal with topics that are of vital importance to a few people, but not to everyone.

But perception applies to *all* of us—male, female, young, old, professional, nonprofessional. It is so much a part of everyday life that we don't even think about it unless we make a point to do so. Perceptions affect our business interactions, our family relationships, our personal lives, our levels of spiritual maturity, and every other facet of life. Nothing is more basic to an individual than his or her *person*-ality.

Therefore, we cannot afford to ignore the problems that exist in our perceptions, nor the opportunities that lie ahead once we learn to better understand ourselves and others. I cannot fully describe the improvements that have occurred for people who have already put these principles into practice. Though I've included a few case histories in this book, you probably won't be completely convinced until you get some firsthand experience. When we learn to eliminate the wrong assumptions we make about other people (and ourselves) and form clearer perceptions of the world around us, things are certain to change for the better.

If you would like to delve deeper into the Birkman Method of personality evaluation, team-building, or other issues discussed in this book, I encourage you to contact us. I hope that in some way, the concepts I have tried to pass along will help you to become a better person, a better boss, a better parent, or a better friend.

May all your perceptions from this point be clear and precise, and may all your relationships grow stronger day by day.

BACKGROUND INFORMATION ON THE BIRKMAN LIFE STYLE GRID

At the time of this book's publication, over 1.5 million individuals had taken The Birkman Method® for personal and professional development.

If you have participated in our comprehensive program and have your own Life Style Grid®, you might appreciate some additional information on the meaning of your personalized grid report.

In the pages that follow are several sample Life Style Grids pulled from the hundreds of thousands in our files. These have been reproduced with the permission of the people to whom they belong, who have in every case fully agreed with our assessment of his or her interests, needs, and behaviors.

A convenient way to present the background information is under the headings of Interests, Effective Style, and Needs and Stress Behavior as separate points on each grid.

Interests

Each category of interest is rated on a percentile scale from 1 to 99. So if a person scores a 92 on the Outdoor category, it means that he or she has more interest in outdoor activities than 91 percent of the other people who have been evaluated.

One advantage of assigning numerical results to the interest categories is to pinpoint areas that may be more than mere interests. We have found that any time someone has more interest in a category than ninety-one of the other people who have been evaluated, it ceases to be solely an interest, and becomes a strong motivational need of the person. When interests reach the "need" level, it is a matter of urgency for the person to find some way to be involved in that interest. If no such outlet exists on the job, the person should seek some type of outside expression at home or elsewhere.

After breaking down a person's interests into separate categories and assigning a value based on how his responses compare with others, *it is then possible to determine a single point on the four-color quadrant that reflects the person's overall position.* We represent this point with an asterisk. And based on what has already been said about the grid, it is a matter of common sense to interpret a person's interests based on the location of the asterisk.

As you will see, merely by adding one more point on the grid for Interests, our four-color grid becomes considerably more complex, with additional points to come. It is as if each quadrant on the grid becomes a separate grid in itself for purposes of comparison and contrast.

If it's been a while since you had geometry or algebra (of if you're much more Green than you are Yellow), you may be a bit thrown by our use of a grid and our expectations for you to think analytically up and down and side to side. Yet it only takes a bit of practice to become quite proficient at using this evaluation tool. We have worked hard to simplify the questionnaire and the whole process involved in the presentation of the results so that you can easily comprehend what you are being told about yourself.

While it is true that personality is extremely complex, it's not quite so difficult if broken down into "bite-size" pieces that can be examined one at a time. First, we pull out "Interests," and further break it down into ten specific categories. Then, after scoring each of the specific areas, the combined results appear as a single point at an appropriate spot on a grid.

On the other hand, you may feel that the presentation seems too simple to be any good. We've put a lot of work into simplifying this evaluation tool. Yet please don't assume that it's *easy* just because it looks *simple*. The only way that something as complex as personality can be represented by points on a graph is that we have honed the process through extensive research and development over decades. We conduct regular validity studies and tests. We make improvements on a regular basis. And as you will soon see, as simple as it may be to understand a single point on a graph, the complexity will come as we add more points, begin to compare an individual's combination of points, and then contrast one person's grid with another person's.

For example, consider the results of the two people below. Since both asterisks are in the Green quadrant, would you say that these people share most of the same interests? It would certainly be correct to assume that they share many of the same interests, yet these two people may not be as similar as you would expect if you were to meet them both in person.

GENE **DEAN**

Gene, on the left, shows an interest almost exclusively in selling, talking, promoting, and working with people (because his asterisk is so far to the right of the Green quadrant). If assigned a job that involved all of those functions, he would probably enjoy and fully participate in those functions. Dean, on the right, also indicates a strong interest in people. However, his asterisk is much nearer the

Red quadrant. So in contrast with Gene, Dean shows more of an inclination for technical activities and practical problem-solving. The ideal job descriptions for Gene and Dean might be quite different, even though both are in the Green quadrant.

Let's try another example. Here are the results of Jan's and Fran's Interest scores.

JAN　　　　　　**FRAN**

Jan, on the left, shows a strong preference for work involving systemization, detail, and mathematics. She would be likely to participate enthusiastically in any activity involving close control of resources, systematization of work flow, or rigid scheduling. At work, she would be well suited for a job that involves intense detail. She is also about as far away from the Green quadrant as she can get, which suggests that she can work independently and requires little interaction with other people.

Fran, on the right, has an asterisk that lies much closer to the Blue quadrant, but not any higher than Jan's. Fran may also work best in an isolated environment. So what's the difference between Fran and Jan? Fran's proximity to the Blue quadrant reflects significantly more interest than Jan's in activities that might require long-range planning, new ideas, and innovation.

Effective Style

On the Birkman Life Style Grid, your Effective Style is represented by a small dot. It may or may not lie in the same quadrant as the asterisk that reflects your interests. For example, suppose someone is a poet. His or her *effective style*—the active behavior—is likely to be in the Blue quadrant. It takes a significant amount of introspection, solitude, and sensitivity to create a beautiful poem. Yet that person may have *interests* that involve lots of other people (Green quadrant). The person may not enjoy being isolated all the time, and would like to cultivate more social interests.

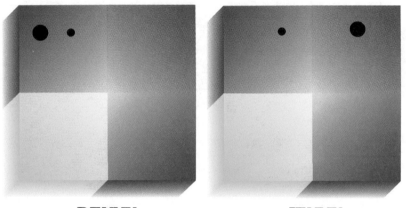

DENNY   JENNY

Now suppose someone is a bank loan officer. His active behavior in the Yellow quadrant makes him appropriately cautious, but his interest is in the Red quadrant, so in other activities he can be forceful and competitive. Similarly, people in any other color quadrants may have interests and effective styles in adjoining or opposite quadrants.

So if you were to see the Life Style Grids of Denny (on the left) and Jenny (on the right), what would you say would be their similarities and their differences?

Both Denny and Jenny should be comfortable with extroverted

communication and direct face-to-face authority relationships. They both appear self-assured, outspoken, forceful, and candid about ideas and opinions. However, Denny is probably much stronger in his beliefs, and his opinions about life and people are likely to be more concrete. His direct, unevasive communication style probably reflects a highly organized and somewhat opinionated value system.

Jenny, on the other hand, is more subjective in her beliefs and attitudes. She may be just as direct as Denny when dealing with other people, but she will be much more sensitive to their emotions.

Now try to evaluate Bill (on the left) and Phil (on the right). Again, try to interpret their similarities and differences.

BILL **PHIL**

Based on the placement of Bill's small dot, he should be most comfortable and effective when using a low-key, respectful, and polite approach toward others and toward work objectives. On the surface, a quiet sociability is apparent along with cues suggesting comfort with order and regulation. Inwardly, however, his feelings and beliefs about people and the world are closer to the internal feelings of someone whose small dot is in the Red quadrant. You might not notice his relatively structured and practical view of people and self if you focus only on his outwardly congenial and cooperative manner.

Phil is also likely to appear quiet, observant, cooperative, and low-key. Yet the location of his small dot suggests that internally he has highly personal attitudes of a subjective and sensitive nature. After a prolonged interaction with him, you might leave feeling as if you had only seen the "tip of the iceberg" of his personality. And you might be absolutely right.

Needs and Stress Behavior

On the Birkman Life Style Grid, we use a big dot to signify the person's needs and reactive behavior. The same point (the big dot) represents both categories, since reactive behavior is based on needs. As we have said, needs are neither good nor bad. All people have needs that can be identified and pinpointed on the grid. And when those needs go unmet, the result is reactive behavior.

The following sample Life Style Grids have been selected to show the wide variety of personality types. At a glance, one can see the results of four major categories: Interests (the asterisk), Effective Style (the small dot), Needs, and Reactive Behavior (both represented by the large dot). As you will see, all of these points fall within the same quadrant for some people. Others have widely diverse points that span the entire grid.

The resulting triangle (or, occasionally, a straight line) on the grid speaks volumes about the person if you know how to interpret the points. A person's Life Style Grid is almost as unique as his fingerprints. We've included just a few comments in each of the following cases. (You should refer to the detailed report that accompanied your grid for additional information.)

JASON W.

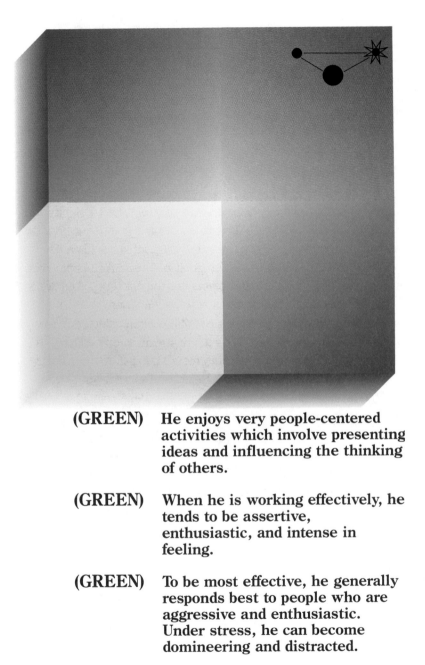

(GREEN) He enjoys very people-centered activities which involve presenting ideas and influencing the thinking of others.

(GREEN) When he is working effectively, he tends to be assertive, enthusiastic, and intense in feeling.

(GREEN) To be most effective, he generally responds best to people who are aggressive and enthusiastic. Under stress, he can become domineering and distracted.

RONNY S.

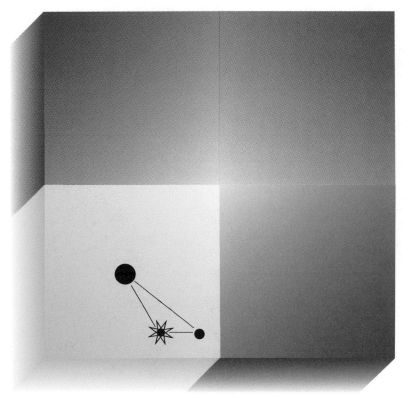

(YELLOW) He enjoys well-defined activities, but he likes to combine these with tasks involving theorizing, planning, or creating new ways of doing things.

(YELLOW) When he is working effectively, he tends to be systematic and reflective.

(YELLOW) To be most effective, he generally responds best to people who are orderly and consistent. Under stress, he may become resistant to change and inflexible.

MOLLY M.

(BLUE)   She enjoys activities which offer the intellectual challenge of discovering, developing, and presenting new ideas and methods.

(BLUE)   When she is working effectively, she tends to be reflective and creative.

(BLUE)   To be most effective, she generally responds best to people who are insightful and persuasive. Under stress, she may become easily distracted and hesitant.

MARTHA H.

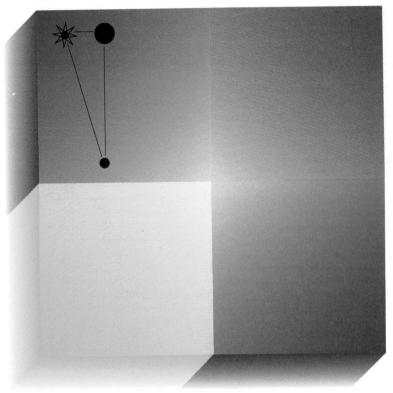

(RED) She enjoys activities with a practical
       emphasis, preferably those which
       offer concrete, visible, and immediate
       results.

(RED) When she is working effectively, she
       tends to be logical and systematic.

(RED) To be most effective, she generally
       responds best to people who are
       objective and decisive. Under stress,
       she may become impatient and
       insensitive.

ANNA M.

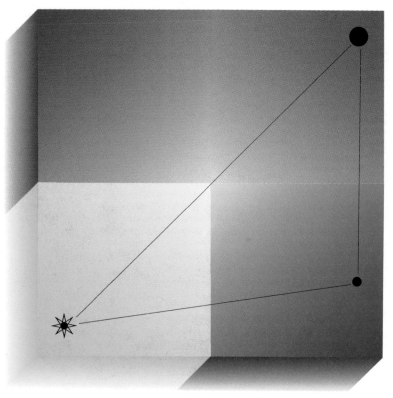

(YELLOW) She enjoys life and work situations which are predictable, reasonably dependable, and secure.

(BLUE) When she is working effectively, she tends to be reflective and creative.

(GREEN) To be most effective, she generally responds best to people who are aggressive and enthusiastic. Under stress, she can become domineering and distracted.

JILL K.

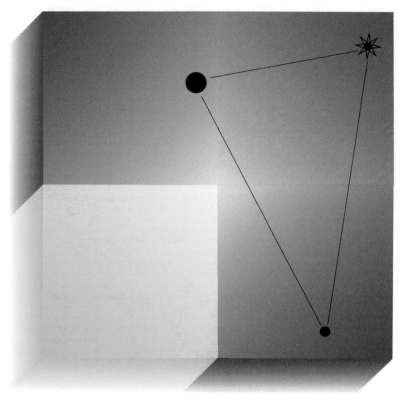

(GREEN)   She enjoys very people-centered activities which involve presenting ideas and influencing the thinking of others.

(BLUE)   When she is working effectively, she tends to be reflective and creative.

(RED)   To be most effective, she generally responds best to people who are direct and forceful. Under stress, she may become insensitive and domineering.

JOHN T.

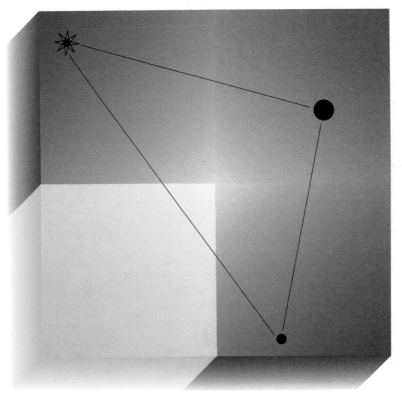

(RED)   He enjoys activities with a practical emphasis, preferably those which offer concrete, visible, and immediate results.

(BLUE)   When he is working effectively, he tends to be reflective and systematic.

(GREEN)   To be most effective, he generally responds best to people who are persuasive and insightful. Under stress, he can become distracted and indecisive.

KALVIN D.

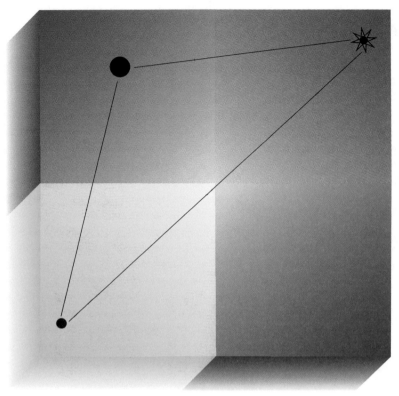

(GREEN)   He enjoys very people-centered activities which involve presenting ideas and influencing the thinking of others.

(YELLOW)   When he is working effectively, he tends to be orderly and consistent.

(RED)   To be most effective, he generally responds best to people who are objective and decisive. Under stress, he may become impatient and insensitive.

JAMES G.

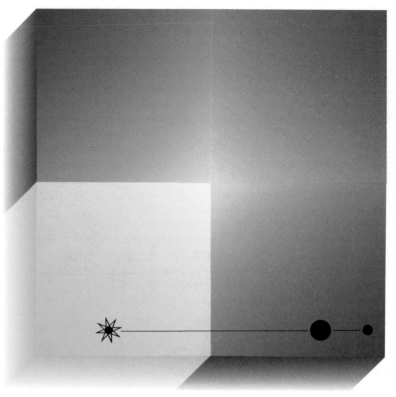

(YELLOW)   He enjoys life and work situations which are predictable, reasonably dependable, and secure.

(BLUE)   When he is working effectively, he tends to be reflective and creative.

(BLUE)   To be most effective, he generally responds best to people who are reflective and creative. Under stress, he can become over-sensitive and hesitant.

JAYNE P.

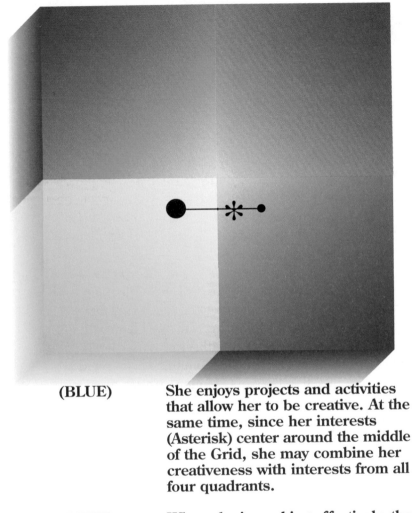

(BLUE) She enjoys projects and activities that allow her to be creative. At the same time, since her interests (Asterisk) center around the middle of the Grid, she may combine her creativeness with interests from all four quadrants.

(BLUE) When she is working effectively, the major emphasis will be on creative aspects because her quadrant interest is in the Blue.

(YELLOW) To be most effective, she has the advantage of drawing on the positive characteristics of the other quadrants. However, under stress, she is vulner-able to stress behavior related to all four quadrants.

SERVICES AVAILABLE FROM BIRKMAN INTERNATIONAL, INC.

Our goal at Birkman International, Inc. is to help individuals and teams communicate and understand. This is most effectively achieved in a group context (businesses, churches, schools, etc.). Only as people understand themselves are they able to relate to others in a group setting.

The process begins when he or she completes a Birkman questionnaire. Through a series of True/False questions, the person responds to statements related to *self*, and then related to *most people*. A short section is for the individual to indicate job preferences by choosing from multiples of four. The questionnaire requires approximately forty-five minutes to complete.

From the questionnaire information, groups learn a *common language* – one that is neither judgmental nor threatening. By separating active (best) behavior from reactive (stress) behavior and needs, people quickly and easily see which areas cause them the most confusion.

It may seem strange that such a simple method could be so precise, yet the results are amazingly accurate. Of course, thousands of hours of hard work, thought, and research have gone into the preparation and improvement of this instrument to fine tune it as a premier instrument for managing behavior and performance.

Our assessment is statistically valid and holds true regardless of age, gender or ethnic culture. We have a staff whose primary function is to ensure the validity of our information.

If you would like to preview what we are able to do for you or your group(s), please visit our web site at www.birkman.com.

THE BIRKMAN METHOD® ON-LINE

Birkman International offers individuals, teams and organizations the remarkable conveniences and power of The Birkman Method® in an interactive Windows™-based system, Birkman 2000ˢᴹ. Birkman 2000ˢᴹ promotes four strategic organizational applications through over 200 on-screen guides:

- **Building Powerful Teams** that will perform with maximum effectiveness and productivity.
- **Selecting For Success** – recruiting and hiring to fill positions right the first time.
- **Coaching For Excellence** and mentoring to help individuals make productive changes.
- **Shaping Successful Careers** that serve both the individual and the organization.

Resources include analytical support and reliable problem-solving direction based on Birkman's archive of national occupational data and experiences. In Birkman methodology, these specifics are illuminated in a wide range of *human narratives and spreadsheets* that allow comparison, what-if simulation, and the actual design of effective development plans and relationships.

Designed to meet the strictest security requirements, Birkman 2000ˢᴹ provides an operational platform specifying tasks and strategic work objectives and designing a plan to fit, or make accurate, informed judgment on both team and individual employee potential, specific conflict resolution, coaching needs and more. Birkman 2000ˢᴹ's lucid Windows™ interface, on-screen guides and *help* system make extremely complex decision making easier. One available Birkman 2000ˢᴹ module, Job Strengthsˢᴹ, as presented on the following pages, is without peer as a team and self management tool.

BIRKMAN JOB STRENGTHS℠

This method of presenting your performance potential serves four color-coded areas critical to your future success and personal fulfillment.

Direct Communication

Expediting   Communicating

Task-Oriented   **People-Oriented**

Administrating   Planning

Indirect Communication

Job Strengths Profiling is the most sophisticated of all Birkman reports. Four General Group scores and 23 Job Family scores reveal an organization's, team's or each person's portrait as unique as individual fingerprints. Each of the Job Strengths profiles is composed of integrating The Method's *55 separate, validated scores*. As a result, it identifies complex patterns of perceptions, work interests, temperament, innate abilities, experiences, habits and unspoken desires that govern motivation and performance which may be totally invisible to managers or colleagues. There is no way to acquire knowledge of human performance to equal the resources of those equipped with The Birkman Method® without years of hands-on work experience.

ANALYZING JOB STRENGTHS

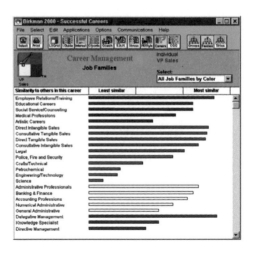

General Groups, *tier one* of Analyzing Job Strengths, provides a framework for understanding the strengths of the organization, team or the individual.

Job Families select, identify or confirm strengths and propensities, and highlight the unique way the organization, team or individual pursues talents, strong preferences, known and unknown.

Ideal Work Environment

RED	YELLOW
–Expediters–	*–Administrators–*

Job Activities Preferred

- implementing
- seeing a finished product
- solving practical problems
- working through people
- organizing

Style

- friendly
- decisive
- straight forward
- logical

Support Preferred

- group interaction
- clear-cut situations
- plenty to do
- logic, directness

When Not Aligned

- avoid giving emotional support
- become impatient
- stay "busy" just to be busy
- dismiss others' feelings

Job Activities Preferred

- scheduling
- handling detailed work
- maintaining close contact
- working with numbers
- developing systems

Style

- orderly
- concentrative
- cautious
- insistent

Support Preferred

- organized approaches
- concentration on tasks
- environment of trust
- consistency

When Not Aligned

- become over-insistent on policies, rules
- resist necessary change
- reluctant to confront others
- may be taken in

Ideal Work Environment

Green
–Communicators–

Job Activities Preferred

- selling and promoting
- persuading
- motivating people
- counseling or teaching
- working with people

Style

- competitive
- assertive
- flexible
- enthusiastic about new things

Support Preferred

- competition
- discussion/debate
- flexibility
- novelty and variety

When Not Aligned

- easily distracted
- distrust others
- become domineering
- fail to follow the plan

BLUE
–Planners–

Job Activities Preferred

- planning
- dealing with abstraction
- thinking of new approaches
- innovating
- developing ideas

Style

- insightful
- selectively sociable
- thoughtful
- reflective
- optimistic

Support Preferred

- individual support
- expression of feelings
- time for reflection
- time for difficult decisions

When Not Aligned

- ignore social convention
- become indecisive
- find it hard to act
- see the worst possibilities

APPENDIX 5

AUTHOR'S NOTE

Material in Chapter 12 reflects the author's perceptions and personal beliefs. However, the basic principles for separating truth from misperception apply to core beliefs common to almost any philosophical preferences. Although this chapter is optional reading, each reader is urged to interpret the statements and observations according to his/her own personal beliefs.

The Birkman Method® Response Form

You may be interested in further information on the benefits of The Birkman Method®. In response to individual inquiries, we are pleased to offer three options to meet the need for in-depth, personal information. Please note that all Birkman relational and occupational Reports are based on information derived from completing The Birkman Method® Questionnaire. To receive your Birkman Questionnaire, please complete the Response Form and designate the Report preferred.

☐ **Option 1 - $45.00**
   Please Circle One of the Following:
   Career Management Report *(General Groups and Job Families analyze your career strengths)*
                     OR
   Color Life Style Grid® Report *(Describes Interests, Usual Behavior, Underlying Needs and Stress Behavior)*

☐ **Option 2 - $195.00**
   Intermediate Report - includes your Career Management Report, Strengths & Needs, Coaching Page and Interest Report *(includes personalized 30-minute taped interpretation)*

☐ **Option 3 - $375.00**
   Advanced Report - includes your Career Management Report and seven Advanced formats *(includes personalized 50-60-minute telephone interpretation with a Birkman Consultant)*

_____Enclosed is my check

_____ Put it on my: VISA / MC (circle one) Card #: _____

   Expiration Date: _____ Name on Card: _____

To assist us in personalizing your interpretation, please provide the following information:

Name: _____

Address: _____

City: _____ State: _____ Zip: _____

Phone: _____

Education: _____ Major: _____

Special Interests, Hobbies: _____

Work History: _____

What are your reasons for completing The Birkman Method®?

   Personal Development   Business Development   Other

Please visit our web site for additional information at www.birkman.com